FROM UNIVERSITY
TO THE SOUTH POLE

MO
**Magnificent
OCEAN**

First published in the United Kingdom in 2013
by Magnificent Ocean
www.magoce.com

ISBN 978-0-9926610-0-7   Paperback Colour
ISBN 978-0-9926610-3-8   Paperback Black & White
ISBN 978-0-9926610-1-4   eBook MobiPocket
ISBN 978-0-9926610-2-1   eBook ePub

Printed in the United Kingdom

Magnificent Ocean policy is to use papers that are natural, renewable and
recyclable products and made from wood grown in sustainable forests.

"Henry took a rare opportunity, and is now sharing those experiences in order to inspire the next generation of explorers (whatever their environment) to dig into the deepest recesses of the self, and then live-out what they might find there."

Dr Stephen Pack
Sport & Exercise Psychologist

WITH CONTRIBUTIONS BY

DAFILA SCOTT
CAPTAIN SCOTT'S GRAND-DAUGHTER

DR DAVID WILSON
EDWARD WILSON'S GREAT NEPHEW
ISCE CHAIRMAN

GEOFF SOMERS MBE
EXPEDITION LEADER

PROFESSOR JOHN SPICER
SCHOOL OF MARINE SCIENCE AND ENGINEERING
PLYMOUTH UNIVERSITY

ANDREW BAKER
DEPUTY EDITOR
TELEGRAPH MEDIA GROUP

DR STEPHEN PACK
SPORT & EXERCISE PSYCHOLOGIST

A percentage of profits from this book are being donated to the Scott Polar Research Institute in Cambridge, UK.

CONTENTS

INTRODUCTION

This book should really be called From University To The South Pole And Beyond as since returning from Antarctica I continue to travel the world visiting hundreds of schools and businesses. I hope to inspire and educate all ages about science and exploration, and of the important role the great expeditions of a bygone age have played in defining our understanding of the global environment.

Before going to university, I spent a year working in various jobs so as to afford a couple of months in the island of Borneo. Exploring the rich ecosystem of the ancient Borneo rainforest and the coral reefs of the South China Sea inspired me to seek every future opportunity to travel and explore.

In 2010, whilst studying Marine Biology at Plymouth University, the International Scott Centenary Expedition (ISCE) headed by Dr David Wilson, the great-nephew of Captain Scott's Chief of the Scientific Staff Dr Edward Wilson, launched a search for one candidate to represent the descendants of the 1912 Terra Nova Expedition in a centenary trek to the South Pole. As I posted my rather hopeful application, how little did I realise what it would all lead to.

Unlike other books of their type, this one comprises of distinct sections focusing on key issues and challenges faced before, during and after I reached the South Pole, with each referencing Scott's own intrepid voyage.

The concepts, struggles and techniques apply equally to many of life's challenges, and if in some way this book helps to inform and inspire you just a little then I shall consider it a success.

Henry J. Evans. 2013

SELECTION

"My Norwegian journey began at 7am on the platform of a cold, empty train station in North West Essex. Over 16 hours later I found myself dining on delicious reindeer soup in a warm, cosy traditional Norwegian lodge, a huge contrast indeed."

Selection Event 3
Sat, 29 Oct 2011

My journey to the South Pole began on the 18th of September 2010 during a visit to the university gym. Whilst approaching the end of a gruelling 10 kilometre treadmill run, an image of the iconic explorer Captain Robert Falcon Scott appeared on one of the television screens. Already a well-known story within my family, having been passed down through the generations, Scott's 1912 Terra Nova Expedition had always been portrayed to me as a perilous journey of incredible courage and fortitude in the face of adversity, and so his image on the screen struck a familiar note. The TV advert was promoting a competition, run in conjunction with the Daily Telegraph, offering a "once-in-a-lifetime" opportunity to join the International Scott Centenary Expedition (ISCE) in a trek to the South Pole; part of a programme of events commemorating the 100 year anniversary

SELECTION

of Captain Scott's great but ultimately fateful journey. Robert Falcon Scott was born and raised in Plymouth, the focal point for the centenary celebrations, and now as a student at Plymouth University I felt an ever closer connection with his story and a wonderful sense of 'place' in terms of British history and exploration.

As a scientist-in-training, in my second year of studying Marine Biology, I was also fully aware of the significant research that Scott's Terra Nova party had conducted whilst in the Antarctic and its continued relevance to us today. I had previously read a great deal about Antarctica as a child and also now as part of my university studies, and therefore knew that this huge white mass of virtually untouched ice at the southernmost part of the world is such a vital place for scientific study. I wrote about this when answering the question in the application process, 'why is Captain Scott important to me?'

After completing and posting my application form, Christmas and New Year came and went spending time with family and friends. In January I returned to university to continue my second year of lectures, coursework, futsal, squash and the usual day-to-day student life and, assuming I had not made the initial selection, soon forgot about the competition.

On the 10th of March 2011 I received an email stating that, as one of the final ten selected candidates, I should report to HMS Raleigh naval base on the 3rd of April. After my initial surprise and excitement, I set about preparing as best I could for what could possibly await us.

SELECTION EVENT ONE
HMS RALEIGH, CORNWALL, UK
3rd - 6th April 2011

HMS Raleigh is the Royal Navy's largest training establishment in Cornwall, UK where Royal Navy recruits receive their basic training. Meeting the other nine candidates for the first time was a memorable moment and I realised immediately that I was up against some tough competition. I found myself surrounded by people from all professions including a glaciologist, a lawyer and an army officer. Each candidate appeared incredibly capable and confident in their own ability. All too aware that I was the youngest of the group, I thought that regardless of the outcome I would at least make the most of this experience and maintain a sense of enthusiasm and purpose throughout.

The officer in charge of us, Lieutenant Cdr Hart, made it clear from the beginning to "remember that we are not looking for the strongest and fittest but for the best possible team member with all that this entails", and that "it was the importance of spirit and teamwork as much as raw strength."

The Royal Navy values of commitment, courage, discipline, respect for others, integrity and loyalty were drilled into us, since these were qualities expected from the winning candidate. Across the four days we were repeatedly physically and mentally tested with new scenarios and activities, with the judges constantly assessing our approach and ability to accomplish each task. They were determined to haul us out of our comfort zone and certainly succeeded in doing so.

SELECTION

Woken each morning in true military style by the sounding of a trumpet call, each day began at 5am with a 'light' run and a session of circuit training. A variety of psychological and physical tests followed, including tackling a muddy assault course and high rope climbing, before the day was rounded off with a stretcher race around the base. Each of us also had to complete a sea survival course, learning how to enter a life raft from a sinking ship, recover an unconscious victim and jump from a high platform into the water.

© Christopher Jones   *Captain Steve Murdoch with the Final 10*

Every event left us feeling utterly drained and aching in all sorts of places. The psychological tests probed our individual personalities, asking us questions such as "what are your life goals?" and "what are your strengths and weaknesses?" Similar exercises to those used for astronaut selection were also conducted to test our ability to remain level-headed when under pressure. This involved being given a series of hypothetical situations and having to communicate our planned strategies out loud to the judges.

© Christopher Jones   *The Stretcher Race*

During our time at HMS Raleigh our writing ability was also tested, since the eventual winner would be required to write a daily expedition blog for the Daily Telegraph website. We were each given ten minutes to write 100 words about our experience over the past few days, before then having to reduce this to a maximum 50 words in an allotted time frame.

SELECTION

My entries were as follows:

"Tired bodies awoke from slumber at 5.30am for punishing early morning fitness drills. High morale was maintained as the team battled like explorers throughout the day, undergoing rowing races, capsize manoeuvres, experiencing the power of ribs and psychometric testing. Every member showed courage and determination, in memory of Scott's achievements."

100 Word Entry
Wed, 6 Apr 2011

"The similar passion of preserving Scott's legacy brought the team together as one, with teamwork forming a vital role in all exercises undertaken. Adrenaline pumping activities undertaken by Royal Navy first level recruits took us all out of our recognised comfort zones."

50 Word Entry
Wed, 6 Apr 2011

Finally, with the event over and our bodies and brains exhausted, it was time to leave the navy training base. We ten candidates had become a tight-knit group, brought together by the strong team work and constant communication that had been vital throughout this challenging experience. It was to be the beginning of a long lasting friendship between us.

FROM UNIVERSITY TO THE SOUTH POLE

SELECTION EVENT TWO
HMS SULTAN, HAMPSHIRE, UK
1st - 3rd September 2011

Royal Navy officer training was up next, held over three days in September 2011. This required us to complete the equivalent of the Admiralty Interview Board (AIB) for Royal Navy officer candidates, which places a greater emphasis on leadership skills.

Two of our initial ten candidates had pulled out by this stage and so we remaining eight were split into two teams of four to take part in a mental agility test. Each team was presented with a military scenario, requiring us to get from 'A' to 'B' using only the equipment provided, such as ropes to swing across open water and wooden planks to traverse over oil drums. Each candidate was required to take the lead in planning a strategy to guide their team to safety, being quizzed throughout on their proposed plan by the assessment board. With only fifteen minutes allowed to plan and explain the strategy to the team, we were then given eight minutes to complete each task.

As my turn came to lead I had a complete mind-blank. Endeavouring to stay calm and focused, and ignoring the sudden quickening heart rate in my chest, I turned to my team announcing "team, I apologise but I haven't managed to solve this one, your help will be needed." Just at this moment, when I was facing potential failure, I suddenly thought of a solution and thinking on my feet guided everyone safely across the water, solving the task in the quickest time. As we shared a team hug I felt a huge wave of relief as by the skin of my teeth I had successfully completed my task.

SELECTION

Further physical and psychological tests were thrown at us and it became a guessing game as to what we would be faced with each day. It was all challenging and exhausting but also exhilarating and I was loving every minute of it.

At the end of our time at HMS Sultan we all said our goodbyes, knowing that this was likely to be the last time we would all be together in these circumstances. Only four were to be chosen for the next selection stage and it seemed to me that any one of those around me were more than suitable.

After a week of waiting and to my huge delight, I was informed that I had made the final four. I was genuinely surprised, but also very excited as I knew we were to travel to Norway for cold weather training. After that the eventual winner would be announced.

SELECTION EVENT THREE
ALTA, NORWAY
28th October - 8th November 2011

Ten days of polar training followed in Alta, Northern Norway which, being 500 kilometres inside the Arctic Circle provided us with experience in a polar environment. It also enabled the realisation of one of my ambitions, to witness the magical Northern Lights. It is truly one of the great natural wonders and one I thoroughly recommend.

> *"A campfire was made and the team spent the evening sat around it, keeping warm and sharing stories. Suddenly a beautiful sight appeared above us as the*

*magical Northern Lights came out to
greet us. A breath-taking sight indeed."*

Mon, 31 Oct 2011

Regardless of any levels of physical fitness, it is training, equipment, local knowledge and experience that prove to be equally valuable in polar expeditions, a point that became very clear during our Norwegian trip. We spent the entire first week learning the essential polar training that I had previously lacked. Lectures were given on pulk packing, polar medicine, types of ski bindings and appropriate methods for layering clothing, together with demonstrations on the correct use of the expedition kit - how to erect a three person Arctic tent and use the stoves and navigation equipment. Considering how crucial all of this is for survival, hours were spent learning the ins and outs of each system. There was also the small matter of perfecting the art of cross country skiing!

Our polar training was then put into practise during a seven day cross country ski across Finnmarksvidda, one of Norway's largest mountain plateaus. This really brought home to me for the first time the demands of a polar environment. Despite having been downhill skiing many times, spending this time trekking and camping in a mountainous region was my first experience of the effort required to manoeuvre even lightly loaded pulks over such uneven ground. However each day, with its long periods of cross country skiing and sledge pulling across icy terrain, became easier and our routine of unpacking and packing the pulks smoother.

© *magoce.com*   Polar Training in Norway

One particular memory I have is when one of the other candidates suddenly fell to the ground while we were skiing, appearing to have twisted his ankle. I immediately switched into survival mode, helping to ensure that the casualty was comfortable and warm as we set about strapping up his ankle as quickly and efficiently as we could. It was only after completing this task that I noticed a rather coy smile on the 'injured' person's face, and that we were also being filmed. The situation had been a set up. I had kept a cool head and dealt quickly with the situation, and so hopefully I had passed the test. It gave me confidence in my ability to react to unexpected situations that could arise at anytime during a polar expedition. It is vital to be quick in thought and action when unexpected situations arise because when operating in temperatures of minus 30 degrees Celsius, as little time as possible must be spent standing still or exposing bare skin.

Each evening, with tents erected and bowls of hot reindeer soup cradled in our hands (which was surprisingly delicious), one of our guides, Geoff Somers, talked to us about his previous polar expeditions and the history of polar exploration. I had heard about Geoff many times before and had also read about his 1989 Trans-Antarctic Expedition. If only I had known then that one year later I would embark on a polar expedition to the South Pole with the man himself.

On nearing the end of what had been ten tough days of training, we were informed that the winning candidate would be announced within a week of our return.

On my return home I looked back on the previous nine months of selection. It had been a fantastic opportunity to be associated with, if only for a short while, such a great British explorer as Captain Scott and to learn more about the Terra Nova story. Throughout the whole process I had been involved with an incredibly friendly, dynamic and hard-working bunch of people and learnt a huge amount about myself. I felt glad to have made the most of the entire experience and to have given it my very best. Equally, and just as importantly, I had had the time of my life and gained invaluable knowledge and experience for the future. Though far from being a fully-fledged polar explorer, this opportunity had definitely equipped me with the necessary skills and knowledge towards becoming one.

SELECTION

Throughout the selection process I had been living two separate lives. On the one hand I was a marine biologist in training, attending lectures, working in laboratories and volunteering at local marine organisations, whilst on the other I was competing as a willing candidate in a competitive selection process.

Both lives required very different skills and knowledge and it certainly made for an exciting and varied time. I could spend a morning in the laboratory dissecting cuttlefish as part of my final year research project and then hurry to an ISCE event in the afternoon, before returning to university in the evening to play futsal and catch up on missed lectures.

On the evening of the 13th of November 2011, I received an email which included the words *'Winner – Henry Evans.'* It was a hugely emotional moment that I shared with my fellow student housemates. The thought of actually venturing to the South Pole had always seemed a distant reality. It had simply been a matter of consistently pushing myself, not placing any limitations on what I felt I could achieve and setting my mind entirely on completing each given task to the best of my ability.

Now, having been announced as the winner, I felt an ever greater sense of responsibility to prove to everyone that I was indeed capable of achieving all that was expected. The transition from student to polar explorer had begun and I was heading for the South Pole.

THE TERRA NOVA EXPEDITION
1910 - 1912

Of the 8,000 men from all over the world who applied to join the Terra Nova Expedition, 65 were chosen. Six of these men had previously been part of Scott's earlier Antarctic Discovery Expedition of 1901 to 1904, including Dr Edward Wilson and Edgar Evans, who later accompanied Scott, Bowers and Oates in their final journey to the South Pole.

CONTRIBUTION BY   DR DAVID WILSON
                 CHAIRMAN, BOARD OF
                 TRUSTEES, ISCE

Commitment; Courage; Discipline; Respect; Integrity; and Loyalty

Water heaved violently in the tiny cabin, knocking the crew off its feet and swirling equipment away into the smoky darkness. The Captain had ordered "brace, brace, brace" as the rockets slammed into the ship; now water was pouring through gaping holes, port and starboard. The gang sought to plug them with techniques as old as the Navy itself. It was hard to bite my tongue and not to shout directions from the viewing platform, as the team struggled to save the ship. This was an exercise designed for Royal Navy recruits in a simulation so real that it soon showed up individual strengths, weaknesses and team virtues. As the ten candidates left HMS Havoc, a ship on rocking stilts to replicate conditions at sea, they had a new air about them. Rather than ten competitors, suddenly they were a team.

I had never intended to be involved in the selection process, not beyond judging the initial essay entries. That much I owed to the Telegraph, which had kindly agreed to back the International Scott Centenary Expedition (ISCE), if we ran a competition to allow a young Telegraph reader to join the team and blog for the paper. The winner had to be literate. Felicity Aston and I went through the entries, the winning ten standing out a mile from all the others. After that, it was over to the physical types to select the winner. Then again, I had never intended to be involved in the expedition in any capacity other than Chairman/Director of the ISCE Board. Political machinations had dragged me more and more into the day to day running in order to keep the project on track and now 'more important matters' distracted the designated selectors, leaving me with another unexpected role.

The first weekend selection at HMS Raleigh was a revelation. Lt. Cdr Paul Hart RN, deputy leader of the British Services Antarctic Expedition (2012) led the weekend with a thorough professionalism. We had linked the ISCE and the BSAE under the banner 'The Spirit of Scott Expeditions', since we shared ideals, and Paul was a huge assistance throughout. The adventurer, Antony Jinman, also led some of the sessions. I was an observer, throughout. From HMS Havoc to the assault course, from pool training to stretcher racing the Navy soon showed its world-class recruitment training. In parsimonious days, however, the Navy is increasingly reliant on private sector companies utilising their team-training expertise in order to maintain it and the splendid coverage of the weekend in the Telegraph gave them just the publicity that they needed. Quid pro quo.

The HMS Raleigh weekend selection left a huge dilemma, however. It was a reasonable expectation that, from ten essays written into a national paper, at least half of the entrants would prove to be unsuitable once put through a rigorous physical and mental challenge. They weren't. Instead we were left with ten strong candidates who had forged themselves into a formidable team. Whilst they were continuously being ranked on feedback from external examiners, there were no clear winners and the obviously weaker candidates still had time to rise to the physical challenge. As a result, the selection process had to be drawn out over the summer. We were looking for something a little bit 'extra', someone who would really use the opportunity to make things happen around the Scott centenary and beyond. Which candidates would take the opportunity and use their initiative to help create the ISCE, over the summer? Who would go into schools? Who would fundraise? Who would improve their fitness, now that they had a better idea of what was involved? Who would generate media coverage and publicity for the Scott 100? A weekend spent hiking and camping on Dartmoor provided another opportunity for physical assessment but the short notice meant that not everyone was able to attend. In the end, the candidate's initiative, or lack of it, over the summer ended up counting for much.

Our selection dilemma was answered by an invitation from HMS Sultan for the candidates to attend the Admiralty Interview Board (AIB), which again attracted splendid coverage in the Telegraph. This is the process used to select naval officers, rather than crew and is impressively rigorous and effective. Two of the team had now withdrawn for other career challenges, leaving eight finalists to attend the AIB. Once again, I was left representing the ISCE. As they went through their challenges, both physical and mental, the field started to spread more clearly. It also became clearer who was finding inner depths to themselves, revealing potential.

I will forever be grateful to the Royal Navy for these and other contributions to the Scott 100 and in particular to the support of Sir Jonathon Band GCB. Not only was their input a profound help in the selection of the Telegraph reader for the ISCE but I also learned a great deal. This polar historian realised the perfectly obvious. That if you really want to understand Captain Scott, go and spend some time with the Royal Navy. They still train officers in broadly the same way to broadly the same set of values. Scott was a naval officer, through and through, and he organised his expeditions accordingly. It was, in many ways, a profound piece of biographical research.

After HMS Raleigh, we totted up the scores from the various assessors of the various events and the four finalists were announced: Henry Evans; Ali Neygal; Kathryn Rose and Joe Woodward. These four would go for ice training in a final selection event to choose the winner. In the end, I organised a ten day trip to Norway, through Per Thore Hansen, with whom I had once been dog sledging. I also arranged for veteran polar traveller, Geoff Somers MBE, to go. I had worked with Geoff many times before on cruise ships. Somehow, the trip came together, and despite an initial lack of snow the candidates were put through their paces. I am not sure that they found it any easier once it did snow! To my amazement, when it was over, the ice leaders were unwilling or unable to choose a winner, there was so little between them. However, from the existing scores, feedback from the ice event and by assessing what we believed each candidate was still capable of delivering for the Scott 100, the Trustees were able to reach a decision: Henry Evans.

So the ISCE was underway. With the support of his alma mater, Plymouth University and other sponsors, we were able to deliver upon the promise of using the event to launch a major education and outreach programme for the Scott 100, bringing the inspiration of polar science and history to a new generation, world-wide. Almost all of it, however, was down to a happy selection. Henry Evans is living up to the hope that all the Trustees, patrons and sponsors had placed in the project and thence in him. Henry is delivering the inspiration of the Scott 100 to over 100,000 students of all ages (and counting) and reaching millions through his press and book coverage.

SELECTION

The naval virtues taught during the training at HMS Raleigh, Captain Scott's values: Commitment, Courage, Discipline, Respect, Integrity and Loyalty, could not have found a more energetic manifestation. What a winner!

Dr D.M.Wilson, 2013

PSYCHOLOGY

"My mental state seems to vary hour by hour; I can feel very sane one moment and then have a bout of complete madness."

Expedition Day 16
Tue, 01 Jan 2013

I had no idea just how strong a bearing my psychological state would have on this expedition, even more so than my physical ability.

On the 23rd of November 2012, a few weeks prior to our departure for Antarctica, I met with Dr Stephen Pack, a senior lecturer in Sport and Exercise Psychology at the University of Hertfordshire. "Fear of failure is generally quoted as most people's concern during expeditions, whereas in fact losing your mind should be the main concern" were his immediate words of advice. Talking with Stephen I realised that, ultimately, in order to be in the best shape for such an expedition, psychological preparation is as important a factor as physical training.

My psyche had already been strongly tested over the past two years during the selection process as we candidates were put through our psychological paces by taking part in Royal Navy psychometric testing, renowned for assessing the personality

21

and reliable nature of an individual. However, in hindsight, no amount of psychological training fully prepares you for the variety of emotions experienced when immersed in such an extreme and alien environment as Antarctica. A landscape famous for its breathtaking beauty and pristine whiteness, it also embodies all kinds of potential hidden dangers to the mind. It was vital when out on the ice that I had full confidence in my own ability to carry out all the various tasks, from lighting the stove to navigating the route. In such an isolated environment even the smallest of doubts can become exaggerated remarkably quickly.

Stephen Pack had explained that these kinds of arduous excursions are often easier the smaller the team and so I felt fortunate to find myself in a team of two. I was more fortunate still that my fellow team-mate was 63 year old Geoff Somers MBE, a highly experienced explorer with a wealth of knowledge of Antarctica. Knowing I would be travelling with Geoff brought a great sense of ease leading up to the expedition, yet also made me acutely aware of how much I had to learn in such a short space of time to ensure as equal and as strong a partnership as possible. Stephen actually found the combination of a 63 year old and a 22 year old on such a trip fascinating, and rather ominously seemed to be looking forward to hearing how we got on!

On the 17th of December 2012 we arrived on the Antarctic continent, landing at Union Glacier Camp on board the gigantic Russian Ilyushin Il-76 aircraft used regularly to transport equipment and personnel to the research bases across the region.

© magoce.com   *Arriving in Antarctica*

"We have landed at Union Glacier! After a four and a half hour flight and a pretty bumpy landing I took my first steps onto the Antarctic ice. It was a pretty emotional moment after a two year journey with the ISCE to get here.

We plan to be here for three nights, spending the days collecting food, fuel and sledges for the forthcoming trek. Tomorrow we plan to test our equipment and make any necessary adjustments in

*full preparation for our flight on the 20th
of December."*

*Expedition Day 1
Mon, 17 Dec 2012*

Due to successive days of bad weather, we in fact found
ourselves on hold waiting for the departure of our final flight to
our trek start point of two degrees of latitude (120 nautical
miles) to the South Pole.

*"It is -7 degrees with a light northerly
wind, which is a sign of bad weather.
There has been heavy snow and thick fog
and so once again we are unable to fly
out today. The weather is looking better
for tomorrow so hopefully we can soon
get started.*

*Yesterday was the summer solstice, the
longest day of the year. From today the
days will begin to get shorter and so I
hope we start the trek soon otherwise
we'll be walking in the dark!*

*There is a sign at base camp pointing
towards London which reads 9,568
statute miles. Whenever I see this I think
of home, family and friends."*

*Expedition Day 6
Sat, Dec 22, 2012*

It became a frustrating period as each morning we would wake up mentally prepared to begin the 120 nautical mile trek, doing a final pack and equipment check and then remaining on 30 minute stand-by to depart subject to latest weather reports.

© magoce.com   *Waiting for Better Weather*

The time window for good weather has to be long enough to enable the Twin Otter aircraft to fly five hours to our drop-off point and then make its five hour flight back to base camp. During this waiting period a radio call was received at base camp informing of an air crash that had occurred 500 miles away. The personnel at Union Glacier were clearly shaken as everyone tends to know everyone else in the area but thankfully, although the plane was seriously damaged, all crew and passengers were fine. It was an unnerving reminder though of the unforgiving environment we were in and heading further into.

This being Geoff's seventh journey to the South Pole, he knew only too well of the importance of having a well-practised routine to help remain focused and safe, and so we spent each day stationed at Union Glacier going over our own routine again and again. To minimise time spent standing in freezing temperatures we needed to be as slick as possible. On one occasion we skied about a mile out of camp and practised the drill of stopping, setting up the tent, cooking the evening meal and then getting into our sleeping bags. By the time we began the actual trek I felt as though I could set up that tent with my eyes closed.

Occasionally Antarctica can be subject to incredibly strong wind speeds and our preparations included regularly putting up the tent whilst envisioning 'gales'. The priority is always to peg the tent down on the up-wind side first to maintain control and minimise any chance of losing it, before then inserting the tent poles. If the tent ever blew away then that is the end of the expedition, with little hope of rescue until the following day if lucky. The danger this posed certainly played on my mind and I had nightmares about the tent blowing away most nights during the actual expedition. Stephen later explained to me that this form of nightmare illustrates the high level of fatigue and poor sleep state I must have been experiencing.

I was deeply saddened to hear of a recent Arctic expedition in which part of the team's tent did indeed blow away with tragic consequences, and my heart goes out to the family and friends of those involved.

FROM UNIVERSITY TO THE SOUTH POLE

At 11.00am on Sunday the 23rd of December the first available weather window finally enabled the Twin Otter aircraft to depart for our intended two degree start point – we were on our way.

After experiencing five hours of the most incredible views of crevasses and glaciers, we were ready to land. However, there was great difficulty in locating a suitable landing area due to extensive sastrugi fields, eventually adding an hour to our intended landing time. A seemingly minor alteration to our plans actually had a pretty significant psychological impact as not only was it now all feeling very real and unpredictable, but our eventual landing site required an extra three mile ski just to reach our pre-planned start point.

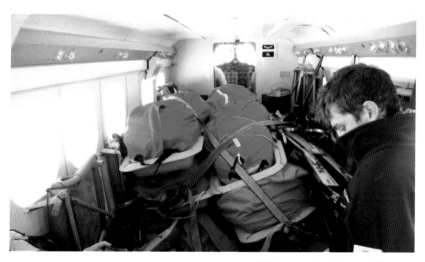

© magoce.com   *Flying to the Drop-Off Point*

And so on this first day we spent a surprisingly hard two hours skiing to reach our scheduled start point before setting up camp. That night the true nature of the task ahead certainly dawned on me and it all felt a long way away from pulling tyres back home.

PSYCHOLOGY

The drop-off had been my first moment of emotional struggle. I was struck by an unexpected wave of loneliness and isolation when watching the plane head back to base camp. We were truly alone, with only our 65kg (143 pounds) pulks and each other for company. Geoff immediately switched into survival mode, pulling off his gloves to retrieve the satellite phone, radioing our revised position to base camp and repacking the phone within a matter of moments. We had not anticipated having to re-evaluate our starting point and so it had been essential to adjust, quickly sort ourselves out and begin ploughing down the miles before the cold set in. "Are you ready for this?" Geoff said. I positioned my skis and poles towards our intended ski direction, attempted an enthusiastic and cheerful response and the expedition really began. Once underway I finally had time to internalise the reality of it all and set my mind to the task ahead.

Setting the right pace through the day is incredibly important and is dictated from the moment of waking each morning. Geoff and I had talked about previous expeditions in which the whole team had to wait for a single member to get ready, thereby leaving everyone else getting steadily colder and so getting the day off to a bad start. Maintaining a well-established routine helps considerably to conserve maximum energy when undertaking such an arduous journey. Stephen had previously worked with another Antarctic explorer who had mentioned expeditions where varying paces had created significant problems.

During the first few days of taking the lead when skiing, I often found myself stopping and turning around to check if Geoff was okay. This clearly and rightly annoyed him as I was wasting my own energy and disrupting our momentum, and so I was told and I took note. It was an indication of my concern at being responsible for us both and also the dependency I felt on Geoff. It quickly became a matter of trusting in my own ability whereupon we progressed to a strong partnership, both relying on each other's words of encouragement and motivation to complete the skiing miles each day.

At the end of each trekking day, we both erected the tent before I climbed inside and arranged its contents while Geoff strapped up the pulks and cut up snow blocks to be melted for water. My test each day was to have a cup-of-tea ready by the time he entered the tent, which is a harder task than it first appears as I couldn't just 'put the kettle on' and even after lighting the stove it takes up to 30 minutes to boil the water.

Christmas Day soon arrived, which we spent skiing in Santa hats, singing Christmas carols and eating Christmas cake in the evening. It was though always going to be a particularly tough day being my first spent away from home.

After spending hours skiing each day at the hands of such unpredictable conditions, it was always a welcome relief to climb into a tent where we at least had some command of our environment. The repetitive routine of carrying out our well-practised procedures also brought a great sense of comfort and a feeling of control, whilst also keeping our focus firmly fixed on the trek itself. The importance of carrying out these daily procedures like clockwork cannot be stressed enough as the end of each skiing day, when feeling cold and completely exhausted, is considered a particularly dangerous period. There is no room for indecisiveness.

PSYCHOLOGY

At times during the day, as my normal senses reacted to the absence of a 'normal' environment, I felt similar feelings to those that I imagine come with solitary confinement. I noticed an exaggerated sense of my physiology, with my heartbeat and breathing sounding so loud that it played on my mind and took several days to get used to. Stephen had stated the importance of retaining a connection both with Geoff and family back home, to help retain rational thinking and keep my mind stimulated.

During each evening meal Geoff and I maintained a light-hearted mood as we discussed today's progress and planned for the next day, before then making a brief satellite call home to relay our

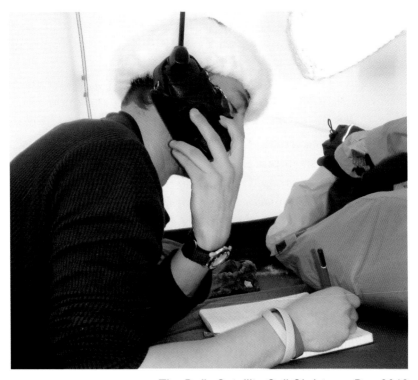

© magoce.com   *The Daily Satellite Call Christmas Day 2012*

30

position and receive any updates. To hear that others were thinking of us was always a tremendous boost and as time allowed, and with great delight, we answered various questions sent to us by followers of the expedition blog.

It is amazing how quickly I began to lose sight of the outside world when immersed in such an immense and unchanging landscape, and so this daily connection with humanity brought a great sense of security.

Over the first few evenings I developed my own routine in the period before sleep. I read letters that I had brought with me written by family and friends and entries from Scott's diary, which he had written during the Terra Nova Expedition almost exactly 100 years before. Looking forward to the simple pleasure of reading another letter or chapter was a real incentive during the day and gave my mind another area of focus outside the relentless thoughts of maintaining ski pace and direction.

As Stephen had advised, as well as having a well-established routine it is also important to be able to adapt to unexpected situations that might arise in such an unpredictable environment. This became particularly evident with the changing weather patterns, which shift very quickly throughout the day from thick cloud to snow storms to a cloudless sunny sky. I found the periods in which the sky was just a mass of white cloud to have the greatest psychological impact. These whiteouts make it impossible to distinguish between where the ice ends and the sky begins, and I could have been skiing upside down for all I knew.

Not having the sun visible for navigation is frustrating and means relying on a chest compass that requires a constant aversion of gaze away from the horizon, the very direction that provides the motivation to keep pressing onwards. At school I had completed the Duke of Edinburgh Gold Award and so already had an excellent grounding in orienteering, but that compass became my least favourite piece of equipment. I found that I became so reliant on the sun that whenever it disappeared my mood dampened a little. Waking up each morning to see bright sunlight streaming through the tent gave a huge boost. It was a real comfort in the sky, warming and urging us on with each step.

Being encased in a sheet of white for hours on end meant the landscape began to play tricks on my mind; cue the hallucinations. Stephen warned of possible hallucinations and feelings of madness so often experienced during polar expeditions, which are in fact viewed as a "healthy and expected experience in such an environment." Such hallucinations are apparently an attempt by the brain to fill in the gaps to provide a detachment from reality. At the time I viewed his advice as interesting, but felt somewhat removed from it as I sat in the comfort of his office surrounded by the all too familiar buzz of university life. It actually sounded a little absurd, and yet, as it turned out, these words became incredibly comforting as his advice turned into reality. Instead of being a shock, these vivid images became a welcome moment of humour to break up the monotony of the ski.

My first hallucination was during the fourth day of our trek when I physically ducked after 'observing' a giant bird flying overhead. These images gradually developed into more interesting observations of mice weaving in-between my skis and a giant sausage baguette suspended in the sky. The baguette was clearly dripping mustard onto the white expanse of never-ending ice in front of me. Initially it was rather scary as I was unsure whether these images were real or not, but they soon became a great way of keeping the mind stimulated. It was all too easy to fall into a blank stupor halfway through the day and think about absolutely nothing for hours. Therefore, to 'see' something other than pure whiteness was a highlight of the day. The fact that these hallucinations were always objects relating to something familiar in the 'real' world brought some rational perspective into this alien environment. Looking back it sounds mad that I was able to extract rational thinking from a floating sausage baguette, but as they say you find comfort in the strangest of places.

Experiencing these hallucinations showed me the importance of keeping the mind stimulated, and so I encouraged myself to daydream in order to add variation to the monotony of the ski. I re-enacted football matches in my head, with a particularly exciting game being a Manchester United v Chelsea FA Cup Final. A 5-4 win to United, thanks to an audacious 40 yard lob from Wayne Rooney in the dying seconds (coincidently I happen to be an avid United fan). It was important to think of anything to ward off thoughts of having to ski yet more miles. Singing also became a notable activity of mine, much to the delight of Geoff, just to hear something other than my own heartbeat and breathing.

When considering that we could walk all day only to stop and camp at a site that looked exactly the same as the night before, it makes sense that the mind evokes elaborate imaginary situations for a sense of variation.

With two days to go before we expected to reach the South Pole, we had a message relayed to us from Sir Matthew Pinsent, the gold medal Olympic rower, who, as a member of a much larger Antarctic expedition some weeks before, advised "not to expect any champagne or coffee or anything at the station as they're a right moody bunch." To be honest I was so focused on reaching the South Pole itself that this thought hadn't occurred to me, but none-the-less I was delighted to receive the message. On starting our final day I was finding things pretty hard going, especially knowing that today we had planned to ski four miles further than our longest daily distance so far. Despite this we pressed on as resolutely as ever, until finally we sighted the faint outline of the South Pole Station buildings. With still some way to go I felt so elated that, as Geoff told me later, I almost ran the last few miles. It shows the incredible power of mind over matter.

On the 5th of January 2013, we reached the South Pole after 14 tough days. It was an incredibly satisfying and proud moment for us both. To stand at the very same spot where 100 years earlier Wilson, Bowers, Evans, Scott and Oates had stood, and as a representative of their families, was a great honour. We raised the flag for the British nation and held a small service of remembrance. It is something I shall remember for the rest of my life.

We found ourselves being warmly welcomed at the polar station, having planned to arrive at a convenient time for the base and also with Geoff being a well-known figure. I found it difficult to wind-down though, and on being handed a bowl of strawberries and cream I thought surely I had noodles that needed to be boiled and kit that needed to be repaired?

Geoff and I shared a great feeling of companionship on this expedition, experiencing each other's high and low points. Considering our varying levels of experience and difference in age, perhaps it would not be expected for us to get along so well and I feel it a great credit to us both in the way we set to the task and helped each other throughout.

After such an experience it is important to have a recovery phase, and so before flying home I decided to spend some time alone camping in the mountains of Torres Del Paine, located in Southern Chile. It gave me the perfect opportunity to rationalise and reflect on the past few months. I considered that if you work hard then opportunities will come your way, and that with the right training and support anything can be achieved. It also made me aware of our incredible reliance upon technology, and thank goodness for it. Without the equipment to communicate our progress and positional data to base camp, our expedition would have been a far more dangerous and risky scheme. This thought brings an ever greater respect for what Scott and his men achieved: True British heroes.

Certainly one thing that helped me throughout was a letter from my Mum, which mentioned the simple words:

"Don't look back, look forward."

It was a mantra that stayed with me throughout the trek, and acted as the perfect motivator.

PSYCHOLOGY

THE TERRA NOVA EXPEDITION
1910 - 1912

It is easily forgotten that setting off for the South Pole in 1912 was like setting off for the Moon in the 1960s.

I can only wonder at Scott and his men 100 years ago, finding themselves exposed to such unusually harsh conditions with nothing but themselves to rely on for their welfare and safety. Imagine Apollo 11 heading for the moon without any contact with Houston Control, finding someone else had landed there first and then returning home, still managing to continue with scientific duties, and then finding yourself in the worst meteor storm ever recorded. It is a wonder they made it as far as they did, and I am so proud to play even the smallest part in promoting their continuing legacy.

Scott's wife, Kathleen, wrote on hearing of his death: "There never was a man with such a sense of responsibility and duty, and the agony of leaving his job undone, losing the other lives and leaving me uncared for must have been unspeakable."

FROM UNIVERSITY TO THE SOUTH POLE

CONTRIBUTION BY   **DR STEPHEN PACK**
SPORT AND EXERCISE PSYCHOLOGIST AT
THE UNIVERSITY OF HERTFORDSHIRE

There are probably very few environments existing today which expose an individual to the challenges that Henry describes as having encountered on his expedition. Therefore, it is a rare opportunity to read about, and consider some of these challenges and reflect upon how they might inform our own way of living. When I first met Henry I couldn't help but think of the opening-lines to the original Star Trek series; 'to boldly go where no man has gone before'. Of course many people have now travelled to the South Pole, including those who enter competitive events. However, this is not to belittle anyone's experiences as these will be unique considering our individual nature, and the rarity of such an environment.

I had spoken to polar explorers before, and heard the stories of competitors in race-events, and they had usually described the psychological issues, rather than the physical issues, as becoming the earliest and most prolonged challenge. But, even though I had some idea of the enormity of his task, and the difficulties he might encounter, I was confident that Henry would cope and flourish. It was clear that he was preparing well, and that he had the demeanour needed to adapt to the challenges that probably lay ahead. But, even though it was possible to predict some of these challenges, similarly to Captain Kirk and his crew, this was to be a journey into the unknown for Henry.

As Henry discovered, and writes about in this book, Polar environments present a rare experience of combined physical and psychological isolation. Many years before Henry completed this book Ernest Shackleton wrote; "in memories we were rich. We had pierced the veneer of outside things…grown bigger in the bigness of the whole. We had seen God in his splendor, heard the text that nature renders. We had touched the soul of man". In other words, polar environments present opportunity for a humbling exposure of the 'soul' to its 'owner'. It is also in such environments that the nature of human resilience therefore becomes most apparent in that people usually do cope with a vast range of challenges such as shock, homesickness, self-doubt, claustrophobia, and again perhaps the biggest challenge of all – the moment of coming face-to-face with the 'self' that the white void can force.

For some these challenges might prove to be overwhelming; but if 'survived' they seem to offer significant personal change in that the environment offers opportunity for a silent mind (as Henry describes). This internal silence, in addition to the probable environmental silence, is something that people have sought for thousands of years in order to live more. The 'ingredients' (e.g. having purpose/s, staying focused on our current task, developing self-confidence, and doing things that gently push us out of our comfort-zone) are one way to achieving a silent mind and are alluded to in Henry's book.

I spoke with Henry on his return from the Antarctic and therefore I've no doubt that he had experienced significant personal change. Most likely any such changes will continue to emerge throughout the rest of his life, and so will be best observed, and commented on, by those close to him. Henry took a rare opportunity, and is now sharing those experiences in order to inspire the next generation of explorers (whatever their environment) to dig into the deepest recesses of the self, and then live-out what they might find there.

Bravo Henry.

Stephen Pack, 2013

PHYSICAL

PHYSICAL

"Geoff and I are both finishing the day feeling physically sick, which shows how hard we must be working. Over the past couple of days I haven't been eating enough and could feel myself wasting away, which has made each of the last two hours feel horrendous. Today I forced myself to eat much more whilst skiing, which has helped a great deal."

Expedition Day 13
Sat, 29 Dec 2012

Trekking the last two degrees to the South Pole requires a cross country ski of more than 120 nautical miles (138 statute miles or 222 kilometres) often over difficult terrain, whilst pulling 65kg of supplies on a sledge. On thinking about this task beforehand, and having read about many of the far greater challenges faced by other explorers, I wasn't overly concerned about my physical ability to complete the distance.

"The SAS take that weight on their back" my friend reminded me for encouragement.

The forces training during the selection process also stood me in good stead, as did the physical assessments at the Royal Navy training bases of HMS Raleigh and HMS Sultan. These had pushed my fitness and endurance levels to their limits, with one particular moment standing out. At one point the candidates were separated into two teams and taken below deck when suddenly, chaos! Lights go out and smoke fills the area as 360 tonnes of freezing cold water steadily pours in through gaping holes and rockets slam into the sides.

© Christopher Jones   *The Navy's Damage Repair Instructional Unit*

A Royal Navy officer in the corner yells "save the ship, stop standing around!" as you fight to fill the holes whilst being rocked violently from side to side. I later found out I had just participated in the dreaded DRIU, (pronounced 'drew' and standing for Damage Repair and Instructional Unit), a renowned Royal Navy physical exertion test.

After being selected as the winning candidate, another year of intense physical training ensued. Geoff and I spent time in the Lake District, pulling tyres up and down the fells to simulate the weight of the sledge we would be pulling during the polar trek.

© Darian Bridge

Geoff and I Training in the Lake District

PHYSICAL

I also completed several half marathons as part of expedition fundraising events, as well as regular weight training and hauling a tractor tyre, lent to me by Tim the local farmer, around the village park to maintain and develop my fitness levels. In the last few months before departing for Antarctica I had hiked to the bottom of the Grand Canyon in the United States, and so overall I felt in great physical shape for the forthcoming challenge.

However, in reality, as many an explorer will testify, perhaps the main physical challenge is not the strenuous nature of the headline task itself but in fact managing to avoid injury and illness, both of which can bring a swift end to any expedition.

Just before our own departure, an extremely well-supported expedition to the South Pole had two team members airlifted out due to illness. I was sorry to hear about this and it made me only too aware that, regardless of physical fitness, we all remain at the mercy of circumstance and the unpredictable polar conditions.

The cold is an ever present danger in Antarctica and exposing bare skin to minus 30 degrees Celsius for just a few minutes can quickly result in frostbite, particularly on the nose, ears, cheeks, chin, fingers and toes. Without constant awareness, carrying out even the simplest of tasks, such as removing gloves to adjust a ski binding or to operate a camera, represent an easily forgotten hazard.

Frostbite is particularly insidious as there is often little warning of its presence until someone else points it out. This became evident with an incident that occurred to the great explorer Sir Ranulph Fiennes just after our return to the UK. When training for another Antarctic expedition, and attempting to fix his broken ski binding at minus 30 degrees Celsius, Ranulph suffered critical frostbite to his fingers which led to his removal from the trip altogether. This brought home the dangers of such unforgiving conditions, and Geoff emailed me immediately upon hearing the news reminding that disaster can strike anyone, no matter how prepared you are.

As part of my own preparations to familiarise with such cold, I spent a day at Millbrook Proving Ground in Bedfordshire. The facility includes a cold chamber, used to acclimatise to polar temperatures and test the suitability and functionality of clothing and equipment. As I made my way into the minus 30 degrees Celsius chamber for the first time, I took a sharp intake of breath and felt the icy cold spread through my lungs. I had never experienced temperatures like it! After adjusting to the initial shock, I practised simple exercises such as undoing zips and taking my gloves on and off. During two 30 minute sessions I also tested the equipment I would be using to conduct a science experiment once on the Antarctic plateau.

As soon as we were dropped 123 nautical miles from the South Pole, Geoff's experience of polar conditions became immediately apparent. "How are your hands?" he asked me, despite being the one using his bare hands to dial the satellite phone and radio our unexpected position in the blistering cold. On landing the temperature was minus 21 degrees Celsius, and so it was imperative to get moving as soon as possible to begin warming ourselves up.

> *"It has begun! This morning was a mad*
> *rush to pack up all the kit, fill the*
> *thermoses and say our final farewells to*

the Union Glacier Camp staff, who we have become very good friends with during the past few days.

We were dropped off 3 nautical miles north of the 88th parallel, which means travelling an extra 3 nautical miles to get to our intended starting point. We then headed south, skiing for 2 hours and covering a distance of 2.5 nautical miles."

Expedition Day 7
Sun, 23 Dec 2012

After trekking for two hours, I was surprised and a little frustrated when Geoff announced that we should make camp for the night. This wasn't the first time though that I found my youthful exuberance being lightly reigned in. I had ignored any thoughts of acclimatisation and in the space of five hours our elevation had escalated from 2,279 ft at Union Glacier to our current 9,000 ft. As I was soon to appreciate, we needed to take time adjusting to this. There was little point trekking for 10 hours a day for the first two days, only to be airlifted out on the third. So for the next three days we gradually increased our daily ski time from 2 to 6.5 hours.

We had previously calculated roughly how many miles we needed to achieve each day in order to reach the South Pole on our intended date of the 5th of January 2013. It was though extremely important that we established a daily ski pace we both felt comfortable with, whilst also meeting our daily target.

The leader is responsible for setting the pace whilst also navigating the way, using the sun and a compass. We took turns to lead, splitting the responsibility into two hour segments in the morning, then one hour and finally 30 minute sessions in the afternoon before setting up camp for the night. It was important to alternate the lead to balance responsibility and so retain an equal partnership. Despite our age gap, Geoff and I shared similar values and we agreed before the expedition that we would only ever ski as fast as the other one was able to.

From a physical perspective, I preferred leading for the first two hours each day when I felt at my strongest, and I was also keen to set the daily pace. I gradually tired throughout the day and it became a real struggle during the final half hour's skiing. We eventually split the final 30 minutes into two 15 minute sections to make it easier; it was though still hell each day.

Avoiding exposure to the elements and ensuring sufficient calorie intake are fundamental factors in staying physically capable of skiing each day's projected distance, and I became only too aware of this early on into the trek.

Experiencing sickness and fatigue after the first few days, due to the effects of acclimatisation, I often didn't manage to eat the entire contents of my snack bag during each break. Geoff and I had specifically weighed out these bags prior to the trek to ensure we received sufficient calories each day. Failing to consume its entire contents meant my body was using up more fuel than it was being fed, and I became more susceptible to the freezing cold environment. I started to feel physically sick in the final two hours of the skiing day, which made the last few miles very difficult. I soon realised that unless I adjusted my eating pattern I would not be reaching the South Pole anytime soon, and so forced myself to eat much more during the day which helped a great deal. Certainly every snack bag from that point on was left completely empty. Simple alterations to the food also made it a lot easier to stomach. For example, we found that preparing the flapjack breakfast the evening before, heating up the solid dry oats on the stove and adding powdered milk and sugar, made the previously solid dry mass far more appealing.

© magoce.com   *Our New Improved Flapjack Breakfast*

By also adding a touch of hot water to the mix in the morning, I found myself eating a surprisingly delicious and, more importantly, calorific porridge for breakfast. It was a small change that made a big difference in maintaining physical condition.

FROM UNIVERSITY TO THE SOUTH POLE

Any slight sign of injury is an unwelcome hindrance to the task in hand and on Day 11 I started to feel a slight twinge in my right Achilles heel. Although I could think of worse problems to experience when miles from help, the lack of focus other than placing one ski in front of the other gave too much time to focus on the pain of each step. The resulting pain also briefly stopped the wild hallucinations which I had come to enjoy and depend upon for moments of mental stimulation.

© magoce.com

Marching Onwards

With the pain worsening, I called Geoff to break for a moment. It was frustrating for us both as the unplanned stop took the momentum out of the ski. I had spent the past three hours battling through, gritting my teeth and trying to focus on the job in hand, but the pain had become too much. It was a welcome

PHYSICAL

relief to find that painkillers were able to ease this for a few hours until we set up camp for the night. Each evening the muscle cramped up but I found that continually stretching it alleviated the discomfort, yet I was still greatly concerned at the thought of it escalating. Thankfully things settled down and caused no further problems.

Each day we began the ski by heading south with backs straight and smiles on our faces, feeling optimistic about achieving more miles than the previous day. Six hours later and the change in our physical nature was remarkable. Hunched over and staring ahead at the seemingly never-ending expanse of ice, we spent the last mile or so longing to stop and collapse into the warmth and safety of the tent.

"The temperature is -26 degrees. It has been sunny all day but with the wind chill it reached -30 degrees at some point.

Another 6.5 hours of skiing achieved, covering a distance of 10 nautical miles. We spent the day skiing into the wind. I had huge icicles hanging off my mask, and when I took this off some of my beard came off with it!

Every single mile we cover I have ever greater admiration for what Scott and his men achieved during the Terra Nova Expedition. What a journey they had. I spent many skiing hours today contemplating how much they endured yet still continued with their scientific duties.

On the 10th of January 1912 Scott wrote:

> *'Only 85 miles from the pole but it's going to be a stiff pull [...] still we do make progress which is something.'*

> *As I sit in this tent now one hundred years on and 80 miles from the South Pole, I so understand the sentiment behind these words."*

Expedition Day 12
Fri, 28 Dec 2012

After spending hours skiing on a smooth and flat terrain, we regularly came across large uneven sastrugi fields, which are piles of wind-blown snow deposits made by snow storms. Skiing through and zigzagging our way around the fields made for backbreaking work as our 65kg sledges often got stuck or tumbled onto their sides. Although tiring, it was also very frustrating as we could spend hours making our way through these fields only to cover a mile or two and so have little to show for our efforts. It was during these times and towards the end of each day that I felt the full physicality of it all.

"Today's quote from Geoff Somers:

*'No one said it was going
to be easy'*

*It has been a very demanding day both
mentally and physically, but I'm pleased
to announce that we are only 0.2 miles
off half-way."*

*Expedition Day 14
Sun, 30 Dec 2012*

When we were only a few miles away from the South Pole, it was necessary to follow strict rules in order to conserve the scientific, environmental, and historical values of the surrounding area. This required us to detour from our firmly fixed southerly bearing in order to join a pre-marked trail, and it seemed very strange to no longer be relying on the sun or compass for direction. The outline of the South Pole Station buildings was now my focus and it felt incredible to be almost there.

On eventually arriving at the South Pole, we collapsed onto our pulks feeling on such a high at the thought that we didn't have to ski anymore. Fear of failure had been a recurring thought in my mind during the past weeks and so it was a wonderful feeling to know we had achieved all we had set out to do.

My first thought on glancing at the plaque marking the geographical location of the South Pole was that I was standing at exactly the same spot where Scott and his men had stood 100 years ago. My second thought was how on earth they had found the physical and emotional strength to set about making the return journey home.

We were flown back to Union Glacier Camp and on arrival I headed straight to the medical centre, or 'Doc's tent' as it is called. She sat me down and checked me over, commenting that I looked "remarkably well and in good physical shape after what you have just endured". No evidence of frostbite, just a well-tanned face and a mangled beard in desperate need of some attention.

The following week, whilst waiting for the flight back to Chile from base camp, I helped to build a huge igloo, played football and French cricket and took part in the first official 'Antarctica Open' golf championships. Clearly my physical shape had not taken too much of a battering. I had though lost over a stone in weight and so set about keeping the camp's kitchen busy.

THE TERRA NOVA EXPEDITION
1910 - 1912

On the 4th of February 1912, Evans took a turn for the worse when he fell into a crevasse along with Scott. It is thought that Evans hit his head and suffered concussion. Scott describes him as being "broken down in the brain". On the 17th of February, Evans stopped to tie his boots and when he failed to catch them up the others skied back to find him. He was found on his hands and knees in the snow. He was put on the sledge and hauled back to the tent. Evans died at 12:30 am, likely from a brain injury brought on by his fall.

Oates followed due to his feet suffering terribly from dreadful frostbite. Eventually his boot had to be cut just so he could get his foot in. He realised that in his appalling state the team would have a better chance of survival without him, and so said the famous words "I'm just going outside and may be some time". His body was never found. Scott, Bowers and Wilson struggled on but by now were low on food and fuel and found themselves in a desperate state. A prolonged blizzard confined them to their tent and they are presumed to have died on the 29th of March 1912.

FROM UNIVERSITY TO THE SOUTH POLE

CONTRIBUTION BY GEOFF SOMERS MBE
ISCE EXPEDITION LEADER

In the history of exploration and adventure there have been the original trail blazers, followed by more adventurers who pushed the boundaries further and even further. The story of the human race has been one of continual exploration, progressing by leaps and bounds, each generation finding new challenges, new methods of overcoming obstacles, eventually turning what was the impossible to the easily attainable.

In the last 100 years, this exploration has moved from the dangerous, often life-threatening venture to being carried out as an often over clinical enterprise where, with our obsession with safety, the fear of litigation should something go wrong, the real meaning of "explorer" has become lost.

Instant communications both with electronic links from and to every corner of the world has allowed the "ordinary" person to undertake projects that at one time would have been considered most foolhardy. Until post the Second World War, anyone setting out on a venture beyond the confines of home boundaries required total self reliance and perhaps some serious risk to life and health. Today, should we "get lost" in the wilderness, there is likely to be the facility to "call in the cavalry", be it by road or air transport. Almost every step of a wilderness journey can be "backed up" and monitored from a home base.

This applies to the polar regions where, each Astral summer, a dozen or more expeditions set out to cross to the North or South Geographic Poles. Aircraft and sophisticated support systems allow the first timer to experience physical and mental challenges quite alien to our cosseted modern existence. To be out of range of instant help, to have to be hundreds of miles from the nearest form of civilisation, can be a daunting prospect. On the Antarctic plateau, in the severe cold and weather systems, living in a small tent, hauling one's own supplies for day upon day, being totally self-reliant, comparatively is as alien to normal life as it was to the hardened travellers through history.

This journey to the South Pole, although just a "taster" – it was not supposed to be a pioneering venture – was still a defiance from the norm and required not just physical resilience but also, a mental adjustment to the isolation, to the vastness of the ice that emphasised our insignificance on this planet.

Each day as we faced into the icy wind and hauled from hour to hour across the never-changing scenery, we would contemplate the journeys of those that went before us, those that, should anything go wrong, there could be no means of assistance. "Lest we forget" as in the epitaphs to the dead in the wars, we would marvel at Scott, Shackleton and Amundsen as well as those others who have almost vanished into obscurity. It was only by "doing" could we really appreciate what had been done before us.

Failure throughout life is always on the cards but perhaps failure itself can be considered as not having a go, not even attempting. As the American polar adventurer titled his autobiography: Dare to Fail, to challenge, to put ones reputation on the line, to be willing to face injury or ridicule, is perhaps the hardest part of all.....

Geoff Somers, 2013

SCIENCE

"The scientific experiment is on-going and so far we have collected 10 snow samples. Each time I collect a sample it takes 10-15 minutes to warm up my hands after exposing them to the Antarctic temperatures."

Expedition Day 10
Wed, 26 Dec 2012

In commemoration of the Terra Nova Expedition and its scientific programme I was keen to conduct a science experiment of my own during the trek to the South Pole, and so with the support of Plymouth University and The British Antarctic Survey an experiment was devised to contribute data towards current climate research.

The project involved collecting surface snow samples every three nautical miles along our traverse from 88 to 90 degrees south, to determine changes in the stable isotopes of water with our changing altitude, latitude and distance from the coast.

Atoms of the same element can have different numbers of neutrons and the different possible versions of each element are called isotopes. Stable isotopes are non-radioactive, or non-decaying, and this stability ensures that any variations are due to external factors. They are an important tool for climate research and comparing our samples against our recorded weather data will enable any correlation to be assessed. Our findings can also be compared against future meteorological data to draw out any significance in the origin and trajectory of the moisture that formed the snowfall.

It was essential to obtain samples from snow directly in front of us in order to avoid us contaminating the area the sample was being taken from. It was also important to collect samples from snow found in the shade to avoid any unnatural interference from the sun when taking temperature readings.

© magoce.com   *Taking a Weather Reading*

FROM UNIVERSITY TO THE SOUTH POLE

Carrying out our investigation during the trek brought a constant risk of frostbite. Every time I took a sample I had to remove my gloves, exposing my hands to the freezing conditions. I soon learnt the best way of reducing the risk - spend as little time as possible exposing bare skin! I devised the most efficient routine during sample retrieval, removing and putting on my gloves at lightning speed and keeping my face downwind at all times.

There is no denying that the trek would have been easier had we not had to stop every two hours to collect snow samples. Reflecting on this, I thought of the vast quantity of scientific samples that were found at Scott's final camp and the demands he and his men made on themselves during their attempted 1,600 mile round trek.

> *"Every single mile we cover I have ever greater admiration for what Scott and his men achieved during the Terra Nova Expedition. What a journey they had. I spent many skiing hours today contemplating how much they endured, yet still continued with their scientific duties."*
>
> *Expedition Day 12*
> *Fri, 28 Dec 2012*

Antarctica has its own beauty, but it is also an incredibly valuable location for scientific research and, because of that, is home to some of the most important and ambitious science projects currently taking place. Largely unaffected by human influence, the almost pristine landscape provides an ideal environment in which to study any natural changes that have occurred over the past hundreds and thousands of years - providing a benchmark if you like, and in doing so allowing scientists to predict possible futures for our planet.

It is the scientific potential of this unique place that is the basis of the Antarctic Treaty. Established on the 23rd of June 1961, the treaty aims to regulate human activity and encourages nations to devote the area entirely to scientific research and exploration. Each year the 50 participating countries congregate for the Antarctic Treaty Consultative Meeting to promote worldwide cooperation in the Antarctic region and discuss the future of the treaty.

This use of Antarctica for entirely peaceful purposes is evident through the fact that the dumping of radioactive waste and nuclear testing is forbidden in the region. However, with areas believed to be rich in minerals such as oil and coal and mined elements including silver and gold, this polar landscape is continually at risk of potential human exploitation. As pressure for these sought-after resources inevitably increases worldwide, there is concern for the continued preservation of this precious and distinctive landscape.

The terms of the Antarctic Treaty hold ever greater importance for the future of Antarctica.

PRESENT DAY SCIENTIFIC RESEARCH

There are currently over 70 research stations in permanent or seasonal operation in Antarctica, conducting scientific research in areas including meteorology, astronomy, marine biology and air pollution studies. During our expedition we visited the aptly named Amundsen-Scott South Pole Station, a US run base occupied by at least 170 people all year round. Here we were able to see some really exciting projects in progress.

AIR POLLUTION

The absence of people in Antarctica means that it has retained a largely unpolluted atmosphere, making it a great place for conducting research into air pollution. It is one of the few places in the world where scientists can research the properties of a clean atmosphere. Some of these studies are conducted in a particular area located close to the Amundsen-Scott South Pole Station, known as the Clean Air Sector (CAS). This site is considered to contain the 'cleanest air on earth'.

Research is also carried out at the Clean Air Sector Laboratory located at the Halley Research Station, a base operated by the British Antarctic Survey. It is here that, using samples of ice cores, studies are conducted into how chemicals in the air become incorporated into the snow. The amount of trapped air bubbles inside each one of these ice cores is measured, and these recordings used to recreate a record of carbon dioxide levels in the atmosphere over the last 100,000 years. The data enables scientists to piece together a picture of past climatic conditions, which in turn can be used to make predictions of future changes in our planet's climate. As a result we can gain an

SCIENCE

understanding of how great of an influence humankind has had on global warming and our dramatically changing climate.

ASTRONOMY

The plateau provides the perfect place for astronomical research. It is an area almost entirely devoid of light and gas pollution with the surrounding high, cold air containing little radiation-distorting water vapour. Since 2007, telescopes have been based at the South Pole Station, looking into deep space in the search for cosmic microwave background radiation. This is radiation created just after the Big Bang and is used by astronomers to determine the age and composition of the Universe.

IceCube is a telescope located at the South Pole at the Amundsen-Scott Station. It is an unusual telescope in many respects. Buried a mile deep in the Antarctic ice, IceCube looks down into and through the Earth rather than up into the sky. The 'light' seen by this telescope is composed of individual fundamental particles called neutrinos. In a real sense, IceCube is opening a new window on the universe and will map the neutrino sky. IceCube will ultimately consist of over 5,100 sensors located in a volume of about one cubic kilometre of highly transparent ice situated between 1,500 and 2,500 metres below the surface. These sensors will detect the optical light emitted by other fast-moving electrically-charged particles (e.g. electrons and muons) moving upward, each of which is the result of a collision with a high-energy neutrino that penetrated the Earth.

IceCube will determine the directions from which the neutrinos, which have no electrical charge and practically no mass, came to us and how much energy each carried. This is a new kind of astronomy, one that hopes to reveal new things about our universe. For example, one of the goals of high-energy neutrino astronomy is to discover the origin of the extremely high-energy cosmic rays that bombard our Earth. It is believed that these neutrinos can be used to identify the sites in the distant universe where these cosmic rays are produced.

© IceCube Collaboration and the National Science Foundation

MARINE BIOLOGY

Marine research focuses on the diverse marine life along the coasts of Antarctica. The fact that its oceans, incredibly rich in biodiversity, are still largely untouched means there are presumed to be many new marine species waiting to be discovered in its deepest depths. It is in particular the adaptations of these species that have enabled them to survive in such cold waters which are of great interest, such as the Patagonian and Antarctic toothfish which produce their own anti-freeze that enables them to survive in sub-zero temperatures. However, these marine species are also a target of the fishing industry and over-fishing has become a huge problem in these waters. Although the Antarctic Treaty has responded by implementing articles to regulate fisheries, the potential destruction of human activity is still a threat. This highlights the importance for future protection of the Antarctic seas in order to preserve the future of its marine biodiversity.

Another area of marine study is the search for microbial life in the frozen waters of Antarctica. These sub-glacial bodies of water are cut off from the normal sources of life such as light and very little heat, and so it is believed that new forms of microbial life, having adapted to their unique environment, may inhabit these deep waters, lying undiscovered for millions of years. These new life forms could provide new research for the evolution of life. While stationed at Union Glacier Base Camp, Geoff and I met members of a scientific team who were carrying out such research into microbial life, as part of a UK run drilling project at Lake Ellsworth, Antarctica. They aimed to drill through three kilometres of ice to reach a sub-glacial lake that, after millions of years of isolation, could contain unique forms of microbial life.

METEOROLOGY

Building on the work that Scott and his scientific team conducted in the Antarctic region over a century ago, meteorology has maintained a central focus at the Amundsen-Scott South Pole Station. Weather balloons are launched daily from the base to record temperature, air pressure, wind speed and the levels of gases such as oxygen and carbon dioxide in the air. These recordings are fundamental to studying the constant changes that are occurring in the Earth's atmosphere, and are used to further research into the ever growing issues of climate change and global warming. These findings can be compared with the measurements taken from the air of densely populated areas to measure the influence human activity is having on the atmosphere. Presently the issue of climate change is a great problem that mankind is facing, a problem that is predicted to continue to escalate in the near future. Therefore, the polar regions play a vital role in our ability to predict our potential future and perhaps even provide answers to change it.

FROM UNIVERSITY TO THE SOUTH POLE

ISCE SCIENCE RESULTS

Background

Water consists of two chemical elements - hydrogen and oxygen.

Hydrogen has two stable isotopes represented as ^1H and ^2H (^2H is also known as deuterium, heavy hydrogen or D).

Oxygen has three stable isotopes represented as ^{16}O, ^{17}O and ^{18}O.

As temperature increases, the quantities of ^{18}O and ^2H in water precipitation also increase. This provides us with a powerful tracer of the Earth's hydrosphere (the combined mass of water found on, under and over the surface of a planet).

This change in the quantity of ^{18}O and D provides an excellent way to retrospectively measure the temperature, date and average rates of snowfall.

The recorded number of stable isotopes found in ice cores is a valuable indicator of climate variability.

Figure 1 below shows two plotted lines:

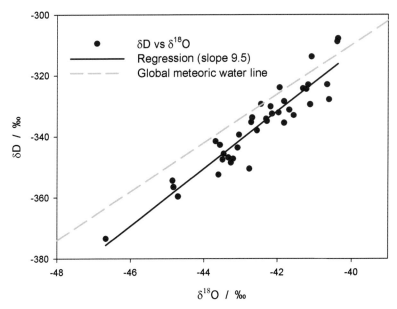

Figure 1: The LMWL results compared to the GMWL
for $d^{18}O$ against dD

Line 1: The Global Meteoric Water Line (GMWL) is shown by the dotted line and represents the expected average combination of ^{18}O and D around the world.

Line 2: The Local Meteoric Water Line (LMWL) is shown by the non-dotted line and is a best-fit of our snow samples collected along the traverse.

The graph plots the local difference, due to the influence of humidity of the source water and the transport pathway, against the expected average.

Figure 2 below shows our snow samples plotted against their latitude from 88 to 90 degrees south.

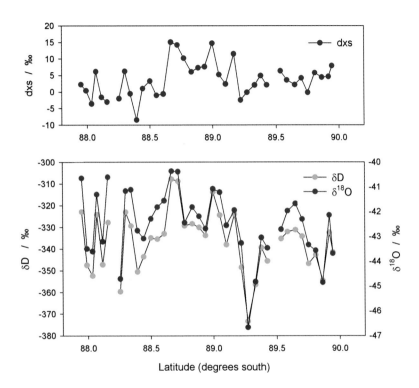

Figure 2:   The variation of dxs, $d^{18}O$ and dD against the latitudinal traverse of 88 to 90 degrees south.

We were expecting to have an easily identifiable correlation with latitude, altitude or weather system, but the results collected prove it difficult to identify this.

The upper plot (dxs) is the deuterium excess. The results give a mean dxs value of 3.5, which can then be compared to the GMWL dxs of 10. These values are related to the humidity of the source. This suggests that the chosen Antarctic traverse had a high relative humidity source.

The lower plot is indicative of the differing air-masses and transport path temperatures delivering snowfall to the sites along the traverse.

There is some evidence here that on the particularly sunny days (24th of Dec and 1st of Jan) we have depleted values. The low values of dD and $d^{18}O$ are possibly an indication of surface sublimation taking place (the process of going from solid to gas), which will preferentially sublime off the light isotopes leaving the heavier isotopes on the surface (i.e. more negative values).

All data are plotted relative to VSMOW2 (Vienna Standard Mean Ocean Water) and expressed in per mile. The values are all negative, showing that the Antarctic water is depleted in the heavy water isotopes compared to the bulk ocean water.

Our data will be added to and compared with existing and future data to help further our understanding of climate change.

THE TERRA NOVA EXPEDITION
1910 - 1912

As well as aiming to reach the South Pole, the Terra Nova Expedition had extensive scientific and geographical objectives. The scientific work was considered by Chief Scientist Edward Wilson as the main work of the expedition: "No one can say that it will have only been a Pole-hunt [...] we want the scientific work to make the bagging of the Pole merely an item in the results."

Described by Scott's biographer, David Crane, as an "impressive a group of scientists as had ever been on a polar expedition", the research these men carried out during their time in Antarctica effectively created polar science as we know it today. The group consisted of various specialists including meteorologists, biologists and geologists, and it was their research that provides the data from which almost every other polar study conducted since derives from.

Using his equipment, considered state-of-the-art for the time, meteorologist George Simpson founded one of the first Antarctic weather stations using weather balloons. We ourselves saw the present day version of these balloons in use at the South Pole Research Station, launched skyward to measure variables such as temperature, light levels and wind speed. During his two year stay at Cape Evans, Simpson conducted these observations whilst also overseeing the running of base camp, having been placed in charge when Scott and his men journeyed to the South Pole.

SCIENCE

Edward. W. Nelson, the shore party biologist, took samples of fish and plankton through holes in the sea ice and conducted tidal observations whilst at Cape Evans. He was also a member of a number of sledging expeditions exploring the interior and part of the search party that discovered the bodies of Scott, Wilson and Bowers in November 1912.

Before joining the Terra Nova Expedition, Nelson worked in Plymouth as a zoologist at the Marine Biological Association (MBA). During my time at Plymouth University, I spent many hours volunteering for various MBA conservation and education projects, which later provided a real poignant personal link during my own trek to the South Pole. A link strengthened by the fact that the MBA also provided the ISCE with expedition equipment.

An integral part to the lasting legacy of the Terra Nova Expedition was Herbert Ponting, the expedition photographer. Scott had firmly believed that the use of photography would enhance the international profile of his expedition. How right he proved to be. Whilst in Antarctica, Ponting spent his time documenting the work of the scientists using a cinematograph, a portable movie camera, to capture short video sequences. He was one of the first men ever to use such a device in Antarctica. The importance attached to documenting this expedition is evident through the inclusion of a tiny photographic dark room in Scott's Hut, an area where Ponting spent much of his time developing his photographic negatives. His photos of the region captured the public's imagination and revolutionised how expeditions of this type were portrayed.

Ponting's footage of the Antarctic landscape and its animal inhabitants still provides us today with evidence that aids the study of the behaviour of indigenous Antarctic wildlife, such as killer whales, seals and penguins. Previous polar expeditions had studied the Antarctic wildlife but the focus had remained predominantly on the Emperor penguin, the animal that to this present day has arisen as the iconic figure of the continent.

Prior to the Terra Nova Expedition, Emperor penguin eggs had never been collected and so little was known about the origin of this species. The struggle to retrieve the eggs by expedition members Henry Bowers, Edward Wilson and Apsley Cherry-Garrard is recorded in a book written by Cherry-Garrard himself called The Worst Journey in the World. The Emperor penguin embryo was the source from which scientists of the period hoped to prove a link between dinosaurs and birds, and thereby providing further evidence to confirm Darwin's 'Theory of Evolution'. At it happened, the study found no link. Emperor penguin skins were also collected to provide control specimens, which half a century later proved that the pesticide DDT had since arrived in the supposedly pristine Antarctic; information that in 1972 helped achieve its ban in the US.

Overall the expedition team collected samples from nearly 2000 species, from which over 400 were found to be of a new kind. A new species discovery rate of 20% is an extraordinary figure and highlights how little the Antarctic landscape had previously been studied. The Terra Nova team were fundamental in confirming the diversity of wildlife in existence.

Geological samples formed a large part of the Terra Nova scientific expedition, particularly evident in the fact that roughly

16kg (35 pounds) of fossils were found lying near the frozen bodies of Scott, Bowers and Wilson by the search party. This evidence highlights how, even to the very end, the scientific aspect of the expedition remained of great importance. Although this decision by the men has attracted criticism, the value of this fossil evidence can be likened to the value of present day moon rock.

Indeed, upon its study the fossil of the extinct seed-bearing tree *Glossopteris indica* collected by Scott was later found to have great significance in confirming the theory that Antarctica had once been part of the ancient continent called Gondwanaland. The fact that this landmass was also known to include South America, Africa, India and Australia and had a tropical climate proved to be a revelation, and changed our thinking of how our planet looked millions of years ago.

FROM UNIVERSITY TO THE SOUTH POLE

CONTRIBUTION BY JOHN SPICER
                        PROFESSOR OF MARINE ZOOLOGY
                        PLYMOUTH UNIVERSITY

Uncovering the 'Secrets of Nature' is often portrayed as the goal of scientific enquiry. But Nature does not yield her secrets easily. Good Science demands considerable thought, ingenuity, careful planning, (some good fortune) and perhaps most importantly, the ability to stick with a task or experiment through the good (10%) and particularly the bad (90%) times.

It is difficult to comprehend until you've tried it but doing Science is really hard work. While the prospect of 'discovery', however small, keeps you going, most of what you actually do often sounds repetitive and trivial. If the process is described in detail at a party it is most likely to render you alone, an abandoned island in a sea of fun. Take Henry's collection of snow samples. Walk for two hours, find an undisturbed spot ahead of, not behind, you and then as carefully as possible take a sample, in exactly the same way each time, taking care to avoid all possible routes of contamination.... over and over again, freezing your fingers off each time. His undergraduate degree would have, to some extent, prepared Henry for all of this, particularly the Honours project and the overseas field courses. Henry and his fellow marine biologists, pursuing their own scientific question and with staff acting as mentors, would work all hours, carrying out repetitive experiments or measurements, spending days, sometimes weeks/months in the lab or field, enduring difficult and trying conditions, all to find out if, for example, fiddler crab behaviour is disturbed by sound, or if barnacle size affected by where the barnacle lives. I suppose at least in Antarctica there were few on-looking locals with 'what on earth is he doing?' smeared contemptuously across their faces.

SCIENCE

And if Science is really hard work then Antarctic Science is very often physically demanding hard work with added exclamation marks. It's interesting that Henry's 'physical' preparation for the trip to the pole, a trip which included those arduous two hourly halts to collect snow samples, sounds very much like Charles Kingsley's description of the perfect scientist, who, "should be strong in body; able to haul a dredge, climb a rock, turn a boulder, walk all day, uncertain where he should eat or rest….and, if he go far abroad, be able on occasion to fight for his life."

So, Science is hard work and Antarctic Science itself is particularly hard work. The question is, is it worth the effort …and expense? For many scientists the thrill of discovery is often the chief motivator. Unfortunately there is now a more pressing reason for doing Science. It is now undeniable we live in a 'World of Wounds', an earth where we are destroying or degrading the biological fabric that keeps us, and all other living things, alive. Antarctica itself is one part of our world where climate change is most marked. And we're only just beginning to discover what this will mean for our own futures and the future of the planet. Much of the scientific work that Henry describes above is interesting in its own right, but it is also key to us predicting our own possible futures – and it is in this context that the seemingly mind- and finger- numbing trivial tasks, like stopping to pick up bits of snow during a walk to the Pole, can become significant, vital and of the greatest importance.

John Spicer, 2013

MEDIA

"Today I had two 30 minute sessions at -35 degrees Celsius in the cold chamber at the Millbrook Proving Ground, during which I conducted simple manoeuvres, such as my science experiment, to prepare for the conditions I will face. After the first 10 minutes, I began to feel the biting cold and so set about warming myself up with swinging arms. The Daily Telegraph reporter joined me in the chamber for brief periods, with him facing his own battle against the chill. Towards the end the penguin costume was brought out, with much cheer from the people watching outside."

18 Days to Departure
Wed, 21 Nov 2012

MEDIA

Arguably the toughest part of any expedition is raising sufficient funds to support it, and so in many ways the ski to the South Pole actually felt like the easier part.

The purpose of the International Scott Centenary Expedition (ISCE) was to commemorate the 1912 Terra Nova Expedition and support an ongoing education and outreach programme to highlight the importance of today's Antarctic science. Clearly a fundamental part of this is to reach out to as many people as possible, and so in the year before our departure a great deal of effort was spent promoting the expedition. It was particularly important that awareness was raised prior to the trek as once in Antarctica we would only have limited (and very expensive) contact with the outside world, and with much of that communication time reserved for daily safety updates.

Media coverage of the selection process itself had already created excellent momentum, and shortly after being announced as the winning candidate an interview was arranged with the BBC. I found myself sitting in front of three cameras, having make-up hurriedly applied and a microphone attached, before launching into a live interview. Drawing on my experience during the selection events, I concentrated on trying to appear confident and in control even if inside I was not feeling quite so at ease. Throughout, I kept reminding myself why I was here. I was now a representative of the ISCE and knew the importance of promoting awareness for the Scott Centenary.

Newspaper articles on Captain Scott's legacy and the preparations for our own expedition followed, with both the Daily Telegraph and BBC websites helping to spread the word. A variety of fundraising events were organised, including a highly successful cocktail evening in Plymouth attended by the local press and many people associated with the ISCE, including Royal Navy representatives and the Lord Mayor and Lady Mayoress of Plymouth. I had the job of personally looking after them throughout the evening and this was both an honour and great fun. I was well aware beforehand of the promotional requirements, but it is still daunting to be thrust into the immediacy of the media world without having any prior experience. It was simply a matter of having to learn on the job and think on my feet.

Dressed in my penguin costume, I embarked on several half-marathon events in the UK with the funds raised from these shared between a local hospice charity and the ISCE.

© magoce.com

*Penguin and Friend Waddling
The 2012 Plymouth Half Marathon*

The costume certainly gave other fancy dress clad runners a run for their money. One such event that springs to mind was when, with us all lined up at the start, a group of men dressed as bananas stood at my side raring to go. I remember thinking to myself that only in a marathon would you find an animal native to Antarctica right next to a tropical fruit. My penguin costume became a kind of expedition mascot and it continually raised smiles and increased awareness for the ISCE - it was indeed worn at various times during the expedition itself for this purpose.

© magoce.com   *Penguin in his Native Habitat*

I will never forget the look on Geoff's face when, while both sitting in the tent, he glanced across my way to see a penguin sitting contentedly eating his well-earned bowl of beef noodles after a hard day's ski.

FROM UNIVERSITY TO THE SOUTH POLE

Many events were held across the UK to mark the centenary of the Terra Nova Expedition. On the 29th of March 2012 I attended a service to commemorate the centenary of Scott at St Paul's Cathedral. This magnificent building was filled with 2,000 enthusiasts of polar science and polar history including academics, politicians, ambassadors, royalty, the foreign secretary, William Hague, and the first sea lord Admiral Sir Mark Stanhope. They were joined by descendants of those men who survived and those who didn't.

The congregation was reminded of how the expedition's sacrifice was not in vain but had had a lasting legacy. The Prime Minister, David Cameron, sent a message saying the men had helped open the world's eyes to the global importance of Antarctica. After Falcon Scott spoke fittingly about his grandfather, Sir David Attenborough read from the last extract of Scott's diary: "these rough notes and our dead bodies must tell the tale." It was a magnificent occasion and it brought home the responsibility entrusted in me by the ISCE.

At a later ceremony for the rededication of the National Scott Memorial in Plymouth I met HRH Princess Anne, who was very interested to hear about the work of the ISCE and our forthcoming journey to the South Pole.

Whilst attending the launch of David Wilson's excellent book, The Lost Photographs Of Captain Scott, at the Wildfowl & Wetlands Trust (WWT) in London, I had the chance to meet Sir David Attenborough and we chatted about our plans and he advised what to expect when out in Antarctica.

MEDIA

As a tribute to the lasting legacy of Captain Scott's own final letter to his wife, Kathleen, a joint competition called the 'Scott100 Letters' project was launched jointly by the ISCE and the WWT. Applicants were invited to write a letter to anyone of their choosing with the aim of inspiring future generations. The judging panel included a number of wildlife experts such as Kate Humble, Bill Oddie, Miranda Krestovnikoff, Chris Packham and Gordon Buchanan, who chose the best 10 letters for Geoff and me to register at the South Pole, before then being forwarded on to their intended recipients. As part of a planned media event, a few weeks before our departure, I visited the WWT's UK headquarters at Slimbridge, Gloucestershire to also sign and collect the chosen letters.

As an international event, the ISCE attracted interest from all over the world as we continued to tell the story of a famous British explorer and our aim to continue his legacy by educating and inspiring others. Further interviews with television, radio and newspapers provided updates on our preparation, both in the physical training and fundraising events.

With each media appearance I gained more confidence, learning to speak a little slower and with greater clarity of purpose and to make the most of the allotted time to promote the message as effectively as possible. During our expedition I was determined to remain as accessible as possible, and so arranged for an on-line expedition map to display our daily progress and for questions to be forwarded for us to answer though our daily blog. The questions received proved an excellent way to share our experience and, by increasing our own contact with the outside world, had the unforeseen benefit of being a great motivator for us.

© *Sacha Dench*

With Falcon Scott at Slimbridge
for the 'Scott100 Letters' Signing

MEDIA

Each evening I uploaded my daily blog via satellite phone to the Daily Telegraph, Plymouth University, Marine Biological Association and the ISCE websites. Each blog described our progress and altering physical and psychological state, and also made reference to entries from Scott's diary during the moments when he had been at a similar location to us. Perhaps one of the most memorable of these blogs, and which still makes my spine tingle when I read it today, is shown below.

> *"In the middle of the fifth hour of skiing something happened that I will remember for the rest of my life. Behind me Geoff shouted out 'Look! Look!' pointing his finger towards the horizon and shocking me from my daydream. In the distance was an outline of buildings, the South Pole Station. It took a few minutes to realise what I was actually looking at. Scott's own description of this moment is how 'Bowers' sharp eyes detected what was a cairn.'"*

> *Expedition Day 19*
> *Fri, 4 Jan 2013*

However we still had some way to go and on the next day, after trekking a further 15 nautical miles, we finally reached the Pole!

FROM UNIVERSITY TO THE SOUTH POLE

100 Years Later　　　　　　　　　　*The Ceremonial South Pole*

　　　　　　　　　The Geographic South Pole

On reaching the Pole, I was astounded by the scale of the Amundsen-Scott base sited there, and even more surprised to come across such amenities as an arts and crafts room, library, sauna and fitness suite. I had taken with me the book Dead Men by Richard Pierce, a novel inspired by the last days of Scott's expedition. I had previously met with Richard, and on his request I was now delighted to place this beautifully written book in the South Pole Station library.

© magoce.com   *The South Pole Library*

FROM UNIVERSITY TO THE SOUTH POLE

We soon returned to Union Glacier Camp where I conducted live radio interviews. Satellite phone in hand and wearing layer upon layer of clothing to keep warm, I trudged to the outskirts of the camp at 4am local time and waited for the pre-arranged phone call. "A big hello all the way from Antarctica" I said, 10,000 miles away from home.

They had also secretly arranged for my sister to join the call, which was a lovely surprise.

> *"Up at 3:30am local time this morning for a live interview on BBC Radio. How surreal that was, being 10,000 miles away from home at the Earth's southernmost continent."*

> *Expedition Day 23*
> *Tue, 8 Jan 2013*

On returning to Chile, I made pre-arranged contact with the Director of the Marine Biological Association (MBA), Professor Colin Brownlee, who at the time was part of an expedition to investigate ocean acidification onboard the scientific vessel, the James Clark Ross. During our call, Colin was off the Coast of Elephant Island near the Antarctic Peninsula. After overcoming a few technical issues, such as signal delay and poor reception, we updated each other on our respective expeditions. What an interesting and informative, if slightly surreal, conversation we had. On returning to the UK, a joint article on both expeditions was published in the MBA News.

MEDIA

Consolidating on the whole media experience, I have come to appreciate how important and often enjoyable a process it can be, but also how essential it is to be thoroughly prepared. I noticed that appearing comfortable and relaxed also helps your audience to be more receptive towards you.

When in front of a camera speaking slowly and clearly is extremely important, as is being presentable at all times. It is indeed often stated that generally an audience remembers far more about the presentation than the content. I have certainly acquired an even greater admiration and respect for news correspondents, who seem so effortless in front of the camera whilst often under great pressure.

FROM UNIVERSITY TO THE SOUTH POLE

CONTRIBUTION BY   ANDREW BAKER
TELEGRAPH MEDIA GROUP

The greatest danger from a media point of view with a project of this kind is complacency - something the ISCE and all involved with it went to great pains to avoid.

It may seem an extraordinary observation given the effort, energy and risk involved - not to mention the finance - but an expedition to Antarctica is not, in itself, an especially newsworthy enterprise. So the first challenge to be overcome with regard to the media is to establish what marks an expedition out from other research based permanently in the area and other exploratory activities.

The ISCE achieved this in a number of ways right from the very start. The "peg" on which all aspects of the story could be hung was the centenary of Scott's expedition, which provided an instantly understandable answer to the question "Why am I reading about this now?"

With the objectives of the expedition established, and the Telegraph's editorial support assured, we were then able to develop a running narrative based on the selection process, with a series of articles profiling the candidates and detailing the arduous tests they had to endure in order to whittle the field down to the winner: Henry Evans.

The focus then shifted naturally and gradually from the initial concept to the specific objectives of the mission, which the Telegraph was able to articulate while also introducing the readers to Henry and allowing him to explain in his own words what had inspired him to set out to take part in the ISCE, and what his personal and scientific objectives were.

As this process continued we were also able - I believe - to assist Henry with a practical crash course in media expectations and how to meet them.

I can only speak from the point of view of the Telegraph here, but we noted with admiration the tremendous interest that Henry was able to stir up among other media outlets both national and local, in print and broadcast media - all vital to raising the profile of the expedition and helping to achieve its goals.

When it came to actually setting out for Antarctica, the focus shifted more to diary mode, and the method of transmission and publication from straightforward communication and newspaper deadlines to intercontinental email and the delights of the blog.

I think the best description of the relationship between the ISCE and the media would be symbiotic, each successfully benefiting from the presence and efforts of the other.

Certainly from the Telegraph's point of view, our editorial support for the expedition provided us with a steady and developing stream of stories with a constant theme but a gradually shifting series of news angles - a valuable resource that could be disseminated across a variety of our news platforms. It also in less tangible terms, enhanced the image of Telegraph Media Group: it was good to be associated with an exploratory enterprise in the finest British traditions.

FROM UNIVERSITY TO THE SOUTH POLE

What the ISCE received from such publicity is not for me to define, but aside from the undoubted benefits accruing to sponsors, equipment suppliers and other benefactors there was also the comfort of knowing that such considerable, admirable achievements would reach a substantial and influential audience.

After all, there is no point doing a terrific job if nobody gets to hear about it.

Andrew Baker, 2013

EDUCATION

EDUCATION

"What a very surreal 24 hours. Spent as much time as possible at the ceremonial and geographical South Pole taking pictures, and even the penguin costume made a much needed run about, much to the delight of the 170 people stationed at the Amundsen-Scott base."

Expedition Day 21
Sun, 6 Jan 2013

On returning from Antarctica, the real work began in continuing the work of the ISCE's education and outreach programme. Within 6 months I had reached an audience of some 2 million people through various media outlets, and personally held talks for over 100,000 people of varying ages and backgrounds at over 70 schools across the UK, Europe, North America and Asia.

Audiences range from primary and elementary school children to students at Eton College, the International School of Geneva and the United Nations school in New York, prospective university students and a ladies speaking society. At one particular venue I found myself addressing the same audience that Sir Ranulph Fiennes had talked to only a few weeks earlier.

Initially rather daunted by the prospect of such speaking events, I now relish them and am excited at every opportunity to share with others subjects that I feel so passionate about.

It is always a privilege to discuss with people of all ages about the importance of education, climate change and the conservation of our marine environment, with amazing facts about the complex nervous system of a starfish and that a blue whale's tongue weighs as much as an elephant!

© magoce.com   *Speaking at a School in Switzerland*

FROM UNIVERSITY TO THE SOUTH POLE

Adapting the content of each talk according to the specific audience or school curriculum helps to maintain a fresh approach to each and every visit. It is an indication of our ever changing world and of the relevance of progressive Antarctic science to humankind, that I find myself regularly updating the content of many talks.

The material we collated whilst in Antarctica, including photos, video footage and diary entries, is invaluable in these talks and helps to provide an insight into the landscape of the region and the workings of a polar expedition. On New Year's Day, during the trek, I embarked on a mad personal challenge to run out of the tent in minus 30 degrees Celsius, wearing not a lot, and proceeded to have a snow shower. The video footage provides the perfect visual demonstration of the seriously biting cold.

It is always very popular when showing our actual expedition clothing, food, science kit, ice from the South Pole and of course the ever popular penguin costume. Audience participation through dressing members up in the polar clothing is always a fun way to bring Antarctica into the classroom or lecture hall.

Of the many incisive and memorable questions I have been asked, some that particularly stand out are:

"If Captain Scott died, why didn't you?"

"Did you see Father Christmas?"

"How did you go to the toilet?"

"Are you still friends with Geoff?"

EDUCATION

"Why didn't you just fly to the South Pole?"

"Did the penguins recognise you in the costume?"

"Have you met Pingu?"

It shows the true global interest in our environment that a worldwide tour of schools in Australia, Canada, China, Germany, Holland, India, Japan, Luxembourg, Norway, Singapore, Sweden, Switzerland, Spain, Thailand, Turkey, UAE, USA and Vietnam is scheduled well into 2014.

The impact that such talks have on the younger generation became apparent to me after a particular session with 50 keen pupils at a primary school in Cornwall, UK. During break-time I watched as they made sledges out of trays and proceeded to pull each other across the classroom, pretending to be the hardiest of polar explorers.

Each talk helps to increase the awareness of Captain Scott's legacy and of Antarctica. It is the determination of Scott and his men and their courage and scientific ambition that provides the real message for inspiring the younger generation of today, just as it did me. Teaching about the importance of the Antarctic wildlife and today's scientific research may perhaps lead to future generations continuing the campaign to protect its future.

Some of the wonderful feedback I have received from my talks is always tremendously encouraging and a true indication of the enthusiasm to learn about the world we live in. Some of these are shown on the following pages.

© magoce.com   *Speaking at a School in London*

"An interesting, engaging and interactive experience for students of all ages. Henry is flexible and builds an excellent rapport with his groups."

"My year 5 class enjoyed working with Henry. He delivered an enthusiastic presentation and left the children keen to find out more about the ocean."

"I can't start to tell you how thrilled we were to have Henry speak. He was truly inspiring and there has been much positive feedback from the students (and staff!)"

"Both teachers and students enjoyed the Skype experience. Henry showed us his food, his clothing and told some amusing stories about his polar experiences. He has provided a wonderful role model for our young students."

Whilst talking to a group of students at the United Nations International School in New York, I fully realised that here I was addressing those who one day are likely to be in a position to have a significant impact on the future sustainability of our planet. I emphasised the importance of protecting the distinctive Antarctic environment and the likely problems we will face even in our lifetime. The enthusiastic reaction I received was incredible and it felt amazing to know that I may, just may, be making a difference.

FROM UNIVERSITY TO THE SOUTH POLE

CONTRIBUTION BY   **DAFILA SCOTT**
                             GRAND-DAUGHTER TO
                             CAPTAIN ROBERT FALCON SCOTT

The legacy of Captain Scott's last expedition to the Antarctic is considerable and continues to this day.

The bravery and courage of Scott and his companions in the face of extreme hardship on the way back from the South Pole in 1912 was extraordinary. In his own words: " for my own sake I do not regret this journey, which has shown that Englishmen can endure hardships, help one another and meet death with as great a fortitude as ever in the past". Scott's diaries describe the difficult journey back from the pole, the sickness and decline of two members of the party (Evans and then Oates) and the exceptionally cold weather they faced when they got to the Ross Ice Shelf. Despite this they tried always to keep up each others' spirits. Scott wrote on March 3rd 1912 "among ourselves we are unendingly cheerful". When Scott's last messages reached England, they inspired a generation of soldiers who had to face the awful circumstances of World War I. Subsequently, for people who have read about the expedition, his words remain a powerful inspiration both to be courageous in the face of danger and hardship, and also to respect and look after your companions.

Captain Scott's expeditions were both scientific and exploratory endeavours. He set out to find out as much as possible about the geography, geology, meteorology, biology and physics of the Antarctic environment as possible and to this end took with him qualified scientists. Some of the studies begun then continue to this day. Much of the long term research is continued by government-backed programmes in countries which are signatories to the Antarctic Treaty – the remarkable international treaty which was set up in 1961 to put territorial claims on hold and to ensure Antarctica is used for peaceful purposes including science and tourism. Our understanding of the Antarctic environment has grown hugely, and in order to understand global phenomena such as climate change, it is important to know how changes at the poles influence, and are influenced, by the rest of the world.

One direct scientific legacy of Scott's last expedition was the founding of the Scott Polar Research Institute (SPRI) in Cambridge in 1920, first headed by geographer Frank Debenham. As a result of Scott's appeal in his last message "for God's sake look after our people", funds were raised to look after the dependants of the polar party, and the surplus funds obtained were used to found SPRI. The work of SPRI encompasses both poles and continues to this day.

"Make the boy interested in Natural History". So wrote Captain Scott to his wife Kathleen while he lay dying in his tent with the blizzard raging outside. This brief message had substantial consequences for the conservation of the natural world. Kathleen was extremely successful in encouraging her small son Peter (only 3 years old when his father died) to become interested in natural history. He was given a life fellowship to the Zoological Society of London for a christening present and introduced to a number of eminent zoologists of the time, but nothing was forced upon him. His mother herself loved being outdoors and sleeping under the stars. Her favourite brother Rosslyn Bruce, a vicar, was very keen on animals and also very good with them, so he probably had an influence too.

Having been encouraged in Natural History studies at school, Peter went on to read Natural Sciences at Cambridge where he also developed a passion for wildfowling which took him out onto the marshes each winter. His mother had also encouraged him to draw and eventually he decided to try and earn his living as an artist. At this he proved very successful, specialising in painting his beloved wildfowl. More and more, however, he realised how much wildlife was declining at the hands of people and he wanted to do something about it. After World War II, he set up the Severn Wildfowl Trust (now the Wildfowl and Wetlands Trust) at Slimbridge and this continues to this day to work for the conservation of wildfowl and wetlands and to bring people and wildlife together for the benefit of both. In 1961, together with others, he founded WWF (the Worldwide Fund for Nature) and later he was also instrumental in bringing about the moratorium on commercial whaling which has brought about the recovery of many whale populations. Throughout his adult life he worked tirelessly for the conservation of the natural world.

It is marvellous that the Antarctic has such a great ambassador as Henry Evans. His enthusiasm and determination to reach as wide an audience as possible is exceptional. By speaking to a variety of people and especially children, he will be able to bring the story of Scott's expedition and his legacy to a new generation.

Dafila Scott, 2013

THE TERRA NOVA EXPEDITION
1910-1912

Robert Falcon Scott was born in Plymouth, UK on the 6th of June 1868. After a successful career as a Royal Navy officer, Captain Scott went on to lead two of the great early expeditions to Antarctica.

His first expedition called Discovery, from 1901 to 1904, included an extensive scientific programme and his first attempt to reach the South Pole. A three man sledging team consisting of Scott, Ernest Shackleton and Edward Wilson reached just 530 miles away from the Pole. After a second year spent refining techniques in Antarctic travel, the expedition returned home to much public acclaim. Scott had captured the British nation's imagination and he soon set about planning his return.

After much fundraising and engaging with the public, Scott returned to Antarctica leading the 1910 to 1912 Terra Nova Expedition. Equipped with greater polar knowledge, a larger scientific force and more superior resources, Scott set out for a more experienced attempt to claim the South Pole for the British people, Queen and country. However, whilst sailing down to Antarctica, Scott learnt that another expedition was also attempting to be the first to reach the South Pole, led by a Norwegian explorer called Roald Amundsen.

The men of the Terra Nova Expedition set up base at Cape Evans, located on Ross Island, building a well-insulated wooden hut that would be home for the next two winters. This headquarters, commonly known as 'Scott's Hut', remains today and has recently been restored by the UK Antarctic Heritage Trust to ensure its conservation.

The team tasked with the final push for the Pole consisted of Scott himself, Dr Edward Wilson (both veterans of Discovery), Henry Bowers, Laurence Oates, and Edgar Evans. After much struggle they finally reached the South Pole on the 17th of January 1912, only to find they had been beaten by the Norwegian team by just 33 days.

© Dr D.M.Wilson

*From left to right,
Wilson, Bowers, Evans, Scott and Oates.
South Pole, 17 January 1912*

On a terrible return journey the entire team perished. Evans died first, having initially suffered from a wound that had failed to heal properly and then experiencing concussion from a fall. Oates soon followed due to dreadful frostbite. On realising that in his appalling state the team would have a better chance of survival without him, Oates so said the famous words "I'm just going outside and may be some time." His body was never found.

Scott, Bowers and Wilson struggled on but, due to earlier slow progress in assisting their companions and battling appalling weather, the men found themselves low on food and fuel and in a desperate state. A prolonged blizzard confined them to their tent and they are presumed to have died on the 29th of March 1912.

On the 12th of November 1912 their bodies were recovered by a search party launched by the team at Cape Evans. According to the rescue party, Scott had flung open his sleeping bag in what was thought to be an attempt to hasten his death. Bowers and Wilson were both in their sleeping bags and appeared to be fast asleep.

Scott's diary provides an incredible insight into the Terra Nova Expedition, describing so clearly both life in the hut at Cape Evans and the highs and lows of the trek itself. Through reading the diary, it is evident that even as their situation began to worsen Scott and his men remained brave and honourable to the end.

FROM UNIVERSITY TO THE SOUTH POLE

Below is the final extract from his diary.

March 29th, 1912

Since the 21st we have had a continuous gale from W.S.W. and S.W. We had fuel to make two cups of tea apiece and bare food for two days on the 20th. Every day we have been ready to start for our depot 11 miles away, but outside the door of the tent it remains a scene of whirling drift. I do not think we can hope for any better things now. We shall stick it out to the end, but we are getting weaker, of course, and the end cannot be far.

It seems a pity, but I do not think I can write more.

R. SCOTT.

For God's sake look after our people.

In 2012 the British nation celebrated these brave explorers in their centenary year of reaching the South Pole, and at the forefront of this celebration is the International Scott Centenary Expedition. Having now spent a month in Antarctica myself, I can just begin to relate to some of Scott's thoughts. This historic story has helped to inspire the ethos I have today: living life to the full, always with a sense of adventure, plenty of humour and with the responsibility to help others. With an emphasis on science, education and exploration, the ISCE is deeply imbued in Captain Scott and his legacy. Numerous expeditions continue to 'race to the Pole' but to race is an adventurer's dash. Scott preferred instead to also execute his programme of scientific, educational and exploration work - as do the ISCE.

AFTERWORD

Centenary celebrations, such as that of Captain Scott's Terra Nova Expedition, happen but once a lifetime and this whole experience has truly been a 'once-in-a-lifetime' opportunity for me.

I had been advised prior to the trek that a common issue with such arduous expeditions is remembering to enjoy it, and so right from the start I had been determined to do so. It proved to be good advice as I can look back at what has been an incredibly fulfilling experience. It gives me a great sense of pride to have represented the International Scott Centenary Expedition and the descendants of such heroic men as Scott, Wilson, Bowers, Oates and Evans.

The words of Falcon Scott are a worthy summary:

> *"I think the important thing my grandfather's story still does is to inspire people. Everything he and his men did, they did properly, to the best of their ability, and I think that's a lesson to us all."*

I write this now as I sit in the wonderful Deichman library in Oslo, Norway. Unbeknown to many, the descendants of the Terra Nova Expedition team and that of the Norwegian explorer Amundsen, who reached the South Pole just before Scott, have a great respect for one another rather than the rivalry assumed. The descendants of these courageous and historic explorers are united by a shared belief in the importance of friendship, education and the conservation of the environment.

I can think of no better way to continue the legacy of these great explorers than by helping to inspire and educate others about science, exploration and conserving the incredible world in which we live.

Henry Evans
May 2013

*To find out more or to arrange a talk for
your school or organisation, visit the
Magnificent Ocean website at:
www.magoce.com*

ACKNOWLEDGEMENTS

As I stood at the South Pole, I was only too aware of how many people had been involved in helping me to get there. Their effort and commitment has been fundamental in making the ISCE such a success. I am so grateful to each and every one of you.

Thank you to Falcon and Dafila Scott for their continued advice, support and encouragement.

Dr David Wilson, the Chairman of the ISCE, for all his hard work. He continues to be a pillar of support and knows that I always have the success of the ISCE firmly placed in my heart.

Geoff Somers for being the best travel companion I could have asked for. Experience, maturity, wit and humour all merged into one, he is truly a great man and one to aspire to.

Plymouth University for their unwavering support during and after my degree, especially to Vice-Chancellor Professor Wendy Purcell, Director of External Relations Jane Chafer and Dean of Students Dr Maureen Powers.

The Daily Telegraph, especially Mark Skipworth and Andrew Baker, for helping the ISCE to reach a wider audience and for giving me the freedom to write.

A huge thank you to our anonymous benefactor for such a generous and important donation.

FROM UNIVERSITY TO THE SOUTH POLE

Professor John Spicer, Professor Martin Attrill and Professor Colin Munn at Plymouth University for their mentoring and guidance over the past four years.

The Marine Biological Association for providing advice and equipment, including a GoPro camera to record some magical footage.

TrackerPoint for providing their communications and tracking expertise.

The Millbrook Proving Ground in Bedfordshire for the use of their cold chamber test facility.

To Blacks for being an excellent kit sponsor and providing all the kit required, even at short notice.

To all our other sponsors, without whom the ISCE would never have achieved all it has, and continues to do so.

To every school student and member of staff who has listened to my talks. Your enthusiasm and enjoyment for learning is infectious!

And finally thank you to my loving and caring family who have supported me every step of the way. I would like to think of the past two years as a true family effort, as you have provided the backbone I have needed to thrive and make this whole experience a success. From proof-reading articles to encouraging me to get outside in the rain to pull tyres, to providing emotional support whilst I was out on the ice, you have been a crucial part of it all.

FROM UNIVERSITY TO THE SOUTH POLE

EXPEDITION MAP

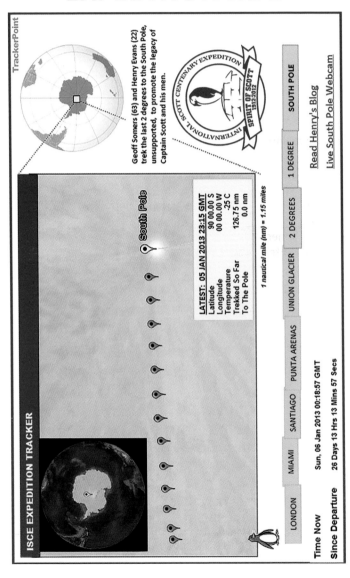

ISCE EXPEDITION TRACKER

TrackerPoint

Geoff Somers (63) and Henry Evans (22) trek the last 2 degrees to the South Pole, unsupported, to promote the legacy of Captain Scott and his men.

INTERNATIONAL SCOTT CENTENARY EXPEDITION

SPIRIT OF SCOTT 1912 2012

South Pole

LATEST: 05 JAN 2013 23:15 GMT
Latitude   90 00.00 S
Longitude   00 00.00 W
Temperature   -25 C
Trekked So Far   126.75 nm
To The Pole   0.0 nm

1 nautical mile (nm) = 1.15 miles

| LONDON | MIAMI | SANTIAGO | PUNTA ARENAS | UNION GLACIER | 2 DEGREES | 1 DEGREE | SOUTH POLE |

Read Henry's Blog
Live South Pole Webcam

Time Now   Sun, 06 Jan 2013 00:18:57 GMT
Since Departure   26 Days 13 Hrs 13 Mins 57 Secs

108

EQUIPMENT LIST

ITEM	QTY	ITEM	QTY
Air Mattress - Self Inflating	1	Solar Panel Charger	1
Air Mattress - Foam	1	Spoon	1
Balaclava	1	Tent	1
Camera	3	Tent Poles	4
Compass	2	Tent Pegs	10
Compass Waist Harness	1	Thermals Upper	2
MSR Stove	2	Thermals Lower	2
Face Mask	1	Toiletry Bags	5
Fleece (Thin)	2	Underwear	3
Fleece (Thick)	2	Windproof Jacket (Outer)	1
Fuel (Meths)	4	Windproof Trousers (Outer)	1
Pair of Gloves (Inner)	1	Water Bottle	1
Pair of Gloves (Outer)	1		
Hand Warmers	25	**PROVISIONS**	**QTY**
Hat	2	Cereal Bars	80
Matches	100	Cheese*	3Kg
Notebook	1	Energy Bars	40
Pee Bottle	1	Flapjack*	4Kg
Pencils	4	Freeze Dried Meals	20
Pulks	2	Hot Chocolate	2
Roll Mat	1	Powdered Milk	5
Safety Pins	20	Salami*	3kg
Satellite Phone	2	Tea Bags	40
Sharpeners	1		
Shovel	1	**OTHER**	**QTY**
Skis	2	Christmas Hat	2
Ski Bindings	2	Penguin Costume	1
Ski Socks	3		
Sleeping Bag	1		
Snow Boots	2		
Snow Sample Tubes	100		
Snow Scoop	1	*for 2	

EXPEDITION BLOGS

DAY 1

MON, 17 DEC 2012, 20:57

(all times are local)

(1 nautical mile = 1.15 statute miles = 1.6 kilometres)

We have landed at Union Glacier! After a four and a half hour flight and a pretty bumpy landing, I took my first steps onto the Antarctic ice. It was a pretty emotional moment after a two year journey with the ISCE to get here.

Standing in the Union Glacier base camp, 2,297 feet above sea level, I am met with breath-taking views of the Ellsworth Mountains, the highest mountain ranges in Antarctica and one of the most beautiful places I have ever been to in my life. It is currently -10 degrees and very little wind so is considered quite warm!

I walked into the dinner tent and was met by the sight of a man reading Scott's journals so I know I'm in the right place. I have spent the last few hours doing some pieces to camera using my tripod and tonight Geoff and I are going for a ski around the camp. We start as we mean to go on!

We plan to be here for three nights, spending the days collecting food, fuel and sledges for the forthcoming trek. Tomorrow we plan to test our equipment and make any necessary adjustments in full preparation for our flight on the 20th of December. However, as is becoming a common feature of the expedition, this is dependent on weather conditions.

DAY 2
TUE, 18 DEC 2012, 21:55

I am currently sitting in snow staring at snow-capped mountains. It is slightly colder today at -12 degrees and still very sunny. This completely pristine environment is a truly magical place.

Slept badly last night as I'm still adjusting to the 24 hour sunlight and the temperature is so changeable throughout the night.

Spent the morning choosing food to last 20 days, which will be needed for our impending trek when we ski the last two degrees. This includes 3kgs of cheese, 3kgs of salami, 120 cereal bars and for the evening, 45 freeze dried meals. Although at the moment these rations are currently looking pretty unappetizing, I can guarantee that we will be so hungry and tired by the time it comes to actually eating them that it won't be a problem.

Went for a 30 minute ski this afternoon and I am pleased to report that no falls have occurred as of yet. It's looking pretty promising!

It is now one week until Christmas Day so make sure you have a mince pie on me. One thing I can be certain of is that I'll be having a white

Christmas. Still expected to fly out on the 20th of December, depending on the weather.

DAY 3
WED, 19 DEC 2012, 20:10

Currently in the tent drinking a cup of coffee. I slept like a log last night, waking up at 4am to blinding sunlight. My body is still very confused. The temperature is -13 degrees and thick fog rolled in this afternoon obscuring the view of the mountains. We are surrounded by dangerous crevasses and so it is important to stay within the boundaries of the base camp.

Geoff and I spent the morning sorting our food into packets per every 5 days. We skied 2 kilometres out of camp this afternoon with our sledges. We will be pulling a total of 120kg across four sledges during our ski.

Also went through a mock camp routine of putting up our tent and playing with the stoves. We cut snow blocks which were then melted for our water supply. I have also been practicing the procedure for the scientific experiment, which we will start conducting tomorrow.

We still aim to fly out at 9am tomorrow and will be given a final weather report later tonight.

The words Scott wrote in his diary the day before he and his team left for their southern journey echo my own thoughts; 'the future is in the lap of the gods. I can think of nothing left undone to deserve success'.

DAY 4
THU, 20 DEC 2012, 14:50

It reached -16 degrees last night and I slept in my thick sleeping bag for the first time, which was very warm and snug.

It is very windy today and so there are no flights out due to the unpredictable weather. We are currently sitting tight until the weather is reassessed tomorrow morning. Scott wrote, 'I can imagine few things more trying to the patience than the long wasted days of waiting'. We are now in that waiting game, with our pulks fully packed and ready to go for when the time arrives.

Our trek starting position will be at 88 degrees and at a height of 11,000 ft. At Union Glacier, where we sit now, it is 2,297ft so this is a significant change and I expect to experience altitude sickness for the first few days.

We plan to ski out this afternoon for more practice. The Union Glacier camp chef gave me some chocolates for us to eat on Christmas Day, but I haven't told Geoff so they will be a nice surprise.

EXPEDITION BLOGS

DAY 5
FRI, 21 DEC 2012, 17:15

It is currently - 10 degrees, feeling warmer with only a light wind.

Yet the weather is more serious nearer the South Pole and so, once again we were unable to fly out. Even though the bad conditions are set to continue into tomorrow, we have to expect a call at any time to be told to prepare to leave.

It is easy to keep busy here at base camp as it feels like one big playground. Today we spent 3 hours crevasse training, learning rope techniques and how to react when someone falls into a crevasse. Our plan tonight is to try and build an igloo.

The beard is steadily growing and in a few weeks should reach an impressive length. The icicles seem to be attracted to it.

There was a very serious air crash in Antarctica yesterday. Thankfully all crew and passengers are fine, but the plane is badly damaged. It is a reminder of the potential dangers in this harsh environment. Everyone here at base camp has been shaken by this news.

DAY 6
SAT, 22 DEC 2012, 18:36

It is -7 degrees with a light northerly wind, which is a sign of bad weather. There has been heavy snow and thick fog and so once again we are unable to fly out today. The weather is looking better for tomorrow so hopefully we can soon get started.

Yesterday was the summer solstice, the longest day of the year. From today the days will begin to get shorter and so I hope we start the trek soon otherwise we'll be walking in the dark!

I spent the morning driving a large snow tractor and chopping up ice blocks to finish the igloo. There are six of us currently working on this project, but it is still tiring work. There are two more layers to go and we plan to spend the evening trying to finish it.

There is a sign at base camp pointing towards London which reads 9,568 statute miles. Whenever I see this I think of home, family and friends.

DAY 7 - TREK DAY 1
SUN, 23 DEC 2012, 23:20

It has begun! This morning was a mad rush to pack up all the kit, fill the thermoses and say our final farewells to the Union Glacier Camp staff, who we have become very good friends with during the past few days.

We took off at 11am local time in a Twin Otter plane feeling rather nervous but hugely excited. It was a 5 hour flight, stopping halfway to refuel at a depot located in the Thiel Mountains. We had spectacular views of 'nunataks'.

30 minutes before drop off Geoff and I kitted up and said our goodbyes to the pilot. It took half an hour to land due to the difficulty in finding a safe location. It was a very bumpy arrival. We were dropped off with our sledges, the plane flew off and suddenly we were alone. I felt very isolated.

We were dropped off 3 nautical miles north of the 88th parallel, which means travelling an extra 3 nautical miles to get to our intended starting point. We then headed south, skiing for 2 hours and covering a distance of 2.5 nautical miles.

It is currently -21 degrees with a light wind. Our position is mapped via the expedition tracker at www.isce.trackerpoint.com.

DAY 8 - TREK DAY 2
MON, 24 DEC 2012, 20:54

Woke up to a temperature of -25 degrees this morning, there was a light wind but not a cloud in the sky.

Due to the extreme altitude adjustment we are building up slowly to the 8 hour ski target for the day. Today we travelled just over 5 miles in the space of four hours. It was very hard work due to the large numbers of sastrugi. We had to zigzag our way around them with the 60kg sledges often getting stuck. Our bodies are getting used to the physical exertion that is required.

On the menu tonight was Beef Stroganoff. Although not the nicest tasting meal I have eaten it did the trick, filling our stomachs and warming our bodies.

I imagine that children (and adults) across the world are getting excited about Santa Claus. I'll be keeping an eye out tonight for my own visit, hopefully he delivers to even the most remote and inhospitable of places!

Tomorrow the Santa hats will be worn by Geoff and me during our ski to get us in the festive spirit. Who knows, we might even sing a few Christmas carols!

DAY 9 - TREK DAY 3
TUE, 25 DEC 2012, 22:05

Ho, Ho, Ho! Well this is certainly the most active Christmas Day I've ever had. It has been an emotional day thinking of family and friends back home, enjoying each other's company and tucking into a mountain of roast potatoes and Brussels sprouts.

This morning we were up at 7am and skiing by 10am. As soon as we woke up the Santa hats went straight on, Geoff and I tucked into some Christmas chocolates and I opened cards from relatives that I had brought with me.

Today we skied for 6 hours, travelling a distance of 8.2 nautical miles. Found the last hour incredibly difficult but battled through it. I led for the first 2 hours, Geoff for the following 2 and then an hour each, before pitching our tent for the night. When leading, you are responsible for navigation using the sun and a compass. It is -21 degrees and we are now 107.67 nautical miles from the South Pole.

I spent the day singing Christmas carols, mainly the classics, 'Jingle Bells' and 'Walking in the Air'. An hour was spent with a Justin Bieber song stuck in my head which, although driving me mad, diverted my focus away from the ski.

My Christmas dinner consisted of prawn noodles, biscuits and a freeze dried Shepherd's Pie (this one really is tasty!). Now we sit here connecting with Scott's own words that 'on Christmas Day, after the feast it was difficult to move.'

I wish you all a very Merry Christmas

DAY 10 -TREK DAY 4
WED, 26 DEC 2012, 21:25

Last night Geoff surprised me with a delicious Christmas cake! Many thanks to Lyn. We are currently finishing off the rest of it whilst sitting in the tent.

It is currently -19 degrees. Today's weather has been variable, starting with thick cloud and it is now sunny with a light wind. Another 6 hours of skiing covering 8.6 nautical miles, being our best distance so far. Tomorrow we plan to attempt 7 hours so let's hope I sleep tonight!

FROM UNIVERSITY TO THE SOUTH POLE

Antarctica is a vast and desolate place and I am realising the impact of being immersed in this more and more as each day passes. The view is always the same, a never ending horizon of white snow and ice, and this starts to play tricks on your mind. I'm almost certain that I saw a bird fly overhead today. I think the hallucinations I've been pre-warned about are already starting!

I'm constantly trying to think of new ways to pass the time whilst skiing. Today I played out an imaginary 90 minute football match, Man United v Chelsea FA Cup Final. A 5-4 win to United, thanks to an audacious 40 yard lob from Rooney in the dying seconds.

The scientific experiment is on-going and so far we have collected 10 snow samples. Each time I collect a sample it takes 10-15 minutes to warm up my hands, after exposing them to the Antarctic temperatures.

I hope everyone enjoyed their cold turkey sandwiches today. Geoff and I have feasted on chicken noodles, chicken risotto and of course the Christmas cake.

99 nautical miles to the Pole and counting.

DAY 11 - TREK DAY 5
THU, 27 DEC 2012, 21:45

A tough day. We pushed ourselves for a further 30 minutes, achieving a total of 6.5 hours skiing and covering a distance of 9.5 nautical miles.

During one of our breaks I shouted out at the top of my voice, 'I AM ENJOYING THIS!' to boost my morale. We have devised a well-practiced system for when we stop to set up camp. The tent is erected and then I throw all the bags in and begin to arrange the tent mat and sleeping mats before lighting the stove. Meanwhile Geoff straps up the pulks and cuts up snow blocks to be melted for water. My challenge each day is to be able to hand him a cup of tea by the time he enters the tent. Today I finally achieved this.

Took some great pictures today. The camera battery spent the entire day down my trousers to keep it warm.

It is currently -24 degrees. Today there were ice crystals blowing from the east. One of the reasons Antarctica is one of the driest places on earth is due to the fact that any moisture in the air immediately freezes, which creates these crystals.

A quarter of the way through, 88.93 nautical miles to the South Pole.

DAY 12 - TREK DAY 6
FRI, 28 DEC 2012, 22:15

The temperature is -26 degrees. It has been sunny all day but with the wind chill it has reached -30 at some point.

Another 6.5 hours of skiing achieved, covering a distance of 10 nautical miles. We spent the day skiing into the wind. I had huge icicles hanging off my mask, and when I took this off some of my beard came off with it!

When the going gets tough I've decided to imagine this trek being my very own Olympic event (except this one seems to last 15/16 days!) or an SAS mission.

Every single mile we cover I have ever greater admiration for what Scott and his men achieved during the Terra Nova Expedition. What a journey they had. I spent many skiing hours today contemplating how much they endured, yet still continued with their scientific duties. Scott quoted on the 10th of January 1912, 'only 85 miles from the pole but it's going to be a stiff pull [...] still we do make progress which is something.' As I sit in this tent now one hundred years on and 80 miles from the South Pole, I so understand the sentiment behind these words.

Geoff and I both feel exhausted so we'll have some more noodles!

DAY 13 - TREK DAY 7
SAT, 29 DEC 2012, 21:30

-29 degrees all day today with a southerly wind directly into our face. We trekked 6.5 hours managing 9.87 nautical miles and I had the biggest icicles hanging off my mask, which looked like fangs. We are currently at an altitude of 10,000ft (nearly 10 times the height of the Eiffel Tower).

Geoff and I are both finishing the day feeling physically sick, showing how hard we must be working. Over the past couple of days I haven't been eating enough and could feel myself wasting away, which has made each of the last two hours feel horrendous. Today I forced myself to eat much more whilst skiing, which has helped a great deal. My snack bag contains a mixture of salami, chocolate and nuts to dip into, though it's necessary to be quick to prevent hands from freezing.

My penguin costume made an appearance in the tent last night and I love how Geoff just carried on as if it was a normal thing to do. Still not quite brave enough to wear it whilst skiing but don't worry I will find a time.

If anyone has a question they would like to ask us then please email it to: isce@trackerpoint.com

Almost at the half-way stage and must keep the spirits up!

DAY 14 - TREK DAY 8
SUN, 30 DEC 2012, 21:35

Today's quote from Geoff Somers, 'no one said it was going to be easy.'

It has been a very demanding day both mentally and physically, but I'm pleased to announce that we are only 0.2 miles off half- away.

We skied the usual 6.5 hours covering a distance of 9.90 nautical miles. Spent many hours singing. Looking back I can't remember what I actually sang, but it was very loud and helped my morale which is the main thing. Poor Geoff!
There were some beautiful cloud formations today, which were changing every minute.

An amazing moment occurred about an hour ago. After complete isolation from civilisation for the past 8 days, a Twin Otter aircraft flew over our heads. I ran out of the tent and stood outside in just my thermals in -27 degrees, frantically waving my arms and with tears streaming down my face. I'm convinced the pilot saw me as the aircraft dipped its wings towards our direction. An incredibly emotional moment. What an experience this is turning out to be.

In answer to one of the questions received today (what are the sastrugi conditions like?) the amount of sastrugi depends largely on the strength of the wind and the direction it is coming from. During our first 20 miles of the trek there were large amounts. However the landscape has been very flat for our last 20 miles, making it a lot easier.

DAY 15 - TREK DAY 9
MON, 31 DEC 2012, 21:30

Coldest day so far at -31 degrees. Travelled for 6.5 hours covering 10.3 nautical miles, which is our furthest distance yet. An amazing boost to morale when getting into the tent and confirming this distance after spending the whole day with our heads down.

The mind definitely plays tricks. Twice today I thought I saw a mouse run under the skis. Once I saw a London bus on the horizon and heard a police siren coming from behind me. After spending 15 days here I realise how everyday sounds are taken for granted.

Have you ever wondered how to make a cup of tea in the middle of Antarctica? First you chop up snow blocks, light the stove, melt the snow, add powered milk and a tea bag and finally, a cup of tea! For dinner we had beef casserole which, as we were starving, was delicious. 50 miles to go now and I wonder if we can do it in 5 days, based on current momentum. When Scott was also this exact same distance away he wrote:

'It is wearisome work this tugging and straining to advance a light sledge. Still, we get along. I did manage to get my thoughts off the work for a time to-day, which is very restful.' I too am finding it incredibly important to drift into deep thought during the day.

In response to a question: 'Are you cold and how comfortable is the tent?' The answer is, if you feel cold then you know you're in trouble, so the only time really is when we stop every 2 hours for about 15 minutes to take snow samples. When walking I feel warm enough. The tent is pretty good as it's quite a large tent for just two of us, but still nothing compared to a bed!

FROM UNIVERSITY TO THE SOUTH POLE

Geoff and I will be raising a glass of Zuko at midnight GMT tonight and thinking of you all back home. Happy New Year!

DAY 16 - TREK DAY 10
TUE, 01 JAN 2013, 21:55

Today reached -30 degrees even though the sun was shining and there were very few clouds in the sky. For the first hour of walking I stayed pretty warm but cooled off during the rest of the day.

We covered 9.9 nautical miles over 6.5 hours. During the third hour of the ski we encountered a huge sastrugi field, which took all of our energy to manoeuvre through and made the rest of the day very hard work.

To celebrate the beginning of a new year I had my first ever snow shower, which involved running out of the tent virtually naked and rubbing snow and ice all over my body before diving straight back into the tent. Although I tried to play the hard-core explorer role I still ended up making a high-pitched scream!

Whilst skiing today my thoughts turned once again to the Terra Nova Expedition. Here we are with a satellite phone and the ability to make daily contact. For Scott and his men, who had no such thing, it only makes their achievements even more spectacular.

Feeling physically exhausted but know I have to dig deeper every day. My mental state seems to vary hour by hour; I can feel very sane one moment and then have a bout of complete madness. However, overall team morale is still very good.

Two thirds of the way through and 40 miles to the Pole!
The question chosen today is, 'any sign of dark meteorites?'
Meteorites tend to collect mainly in the southern mountain ranges, which are hundreds of miles away from us. Were we to find a meteorite a permit is needed to collect one, and any findings reported and location noted.

DAY 17 - TREK DAY 11
WED, 02 JAN 2013, 21:45

Woke to thick cloud this morning, which surrounded the entire tent, and the sun was nowhere in sight. As a result we had to navigate by compass the entire day, travelling for 6.5 hours and covering 9.02 nautical miles.

The view was a sheet of white all around us, making it impossible to distinguish between where the ice ended and the sky began. The hallucinations were more apparent than ever! The most vivid was a giant sausage and bacon baguette floating in the sky. I write this as I tuck into the traditional meal of noodles.

Over the past few days I've had difficulty with my right Achilles heel. After the first 4 hours skiing today, I took some painkillers to try and ease the pain. When I was struggling I focused on Scott and his men, which put things into perspective and enabled me to push on. Scott wrote on the 14th of January 1912. 'It is an effort to keep up the double figures, but if we can do another four marches we ought to get through. It is going to be a close thing.' My back became straighter and I looked straight ahead with renewed vigour. The temperature started at -16 degrees this morning and within the space of 7 hours had dropped to -26 degrees. Almost three quarters of the way now with just 31 miles to go. Hope to arrive at the South Pole in the next three days.

One of the questions received today was, 'how do you secure the tent?' As with any other tent, guy lines are used to secure it to the ground. Our skis, ski poles and walking poles are used to tie the tent down. Valances, bits of canvas, are then placed at the base of the tent and snow pushed against them.

DAY 18 - TREK DAY 12
THU, 03 JAN 2013, 21:40

The tent was packed and we set off 20 minutes earlier than usual this morning. We must be keen to get going!

Skied for another 6.5 hours, covering a distance of 9.9 nautical miles. Grit and determination got us through the day, which felt like the longest of the expedition so far. This is usually a sign that we are nearing our destination. At one point this morning, thinking that surely another hour had passed, it turned out we hadn't even skied for 15 minutes.

Strong wind from the south into our faces this morning, which eased off throughout the day. We hit a few patches of sastrugi but overall the terrain remained relatively flat. Our sledges will be much lighter now than when we started, but I am yet to notice this benefit.

Have had some very strange dreams over the past two weeks and last night was no exception. I dreamt that I was announced as the newest member of Take That and spent the evening having dinner with Gary Barlow. Dream interpreters, good luck with that one!

Currently very warm in the tent having dinner, is it really -30 degrees outside? We are 21 miles from the Pole. We'll keep pushing on.

The question chosen today was, 'what are you using to collect the snow samples?' We use a small vial to collect a surface snow sample every 3 miles, which is per 2 hours of skiing time. We collect 3 samples a day and aim to gather 40-50 samples over the duration of the trek, which the British Antarctic Survey will analyse on our return.

DAY 19 - TREK DAY 13
FRI, 04 JAN 2013, 21:23

It is currently -26 degrees. We have travelled 6.5 hours covering a distance of 9.64 nautical miles.

A day of two halves. This morning we had glorious weather, sunny with little wind and a flat surface to ski on. Even Geoff said 'it doesn't get much better than this'. The sky was a beautiful deep blue gradually getting lighter towards the horizon. Mesmerizing indeed and at times I wasn't even thinking about the fact I was skiing. Our feelings were reflected by Scott on the 16th of January 1912 as he wrote, 'we started off in high spirits in the afternoon, feeling that tomorrow would see us at our destination.'

However, Antarctica is full of surprises and for the next 4 hours we were locked in battle with some of the worst sastrugi we have come across so far on the trip. Very, very tiring but most of all frustrating, with the sledges getting stuck and pulling on the harnesses.

In the middle of the fifth hour of skiing, something happened that I will remember for the rest of my life. Behind me Geoff shouted out 'Look! Look!' pointing his finger towards the horizon and shocking me from my daydream. In the distance was an outline of buildings, the South Pole Station. It took a few minutes to realise what I was actually looking at. Scott's own description of this moment is how 'Bowers' sharp eyes detected what was a cairn.'

12 miles from the South Pole. Final push begins tomorrow.

DAY 20 - TREK DAY 14
SAT, 05 JAN 2013, 23:15

The ISCE team is at the South Pole!

After a 10 hour ski, Geoff and I made it just after 22:00 GMT feeling absolutely exhausted and hugely emotional. Today we covered almost 15 nautical miles, more than expected due to an American requirement to follow a specific route.

Suddenly I'm sitting in a chair with a cup of tea and cookies, surrounded by people asking us about our trek. I realised I had forgotten how to talk to other people. We are surrounded by a mass of activity; a Twin Otter aircraft has just landed.

I'm then told we are off to visit the ceremonial and geographical poles and so we have little time to gather our thoughts. Photos are taken. At 00:30 GMT we are to be given a tour of the South Pole station.

Sleeping in a tent by myself tonight, bigger than the one Geoff and I have both shared for the past two weeks. Complete luxury.

The plan is to fly back to Union Glacier tomorrow.

Scott wrote on realising they were not the first to the Pole, 'many thoughts come and much discussion have we had. All the day dreams must go; it will be a wearisome return.'

Just skiing the last 2 degrees is the toughest thing I've ever done in my life. I am so proud to be part of the ISCE team, and so honoured to be part of this experience.

DAY 21

SUN, 06 JAN 2013, 22:53

What a very surreal 24 hours. Spent as much time as possible at the ceremonial and geographical South Pole taking pictures and the penguin costume even made a much needed run about, much to the delight of the 170 people stationed at the Amundsen-Scott base.

The tour of the base was amazing with some very unexpected facilities such as an indoor sports court, gymnasium and an arts and crafts room. Having just had a shower I now feel like a new man!

Having been awake for 20 hours, I slept soundly last night for 6 hours before being woken for breakfast. We said our final farewells to the South Pole and its residents, and then the ISCE team was back in a Twin Otter plane for a 5 hour flight back to Union Glacier.

The plan is to fly back to Punta Arenas on the 10th of January. Flight back to the UK is on 21st of January and we are looking forward to being reunited with family and friends. I still can't quite believe what an experience the past two weeks has been.

DAY 22
MON, 07 JAN 2013, 16:07

Geoff and I were welcomed back to Union Glacier Base Camp.

Slept for 11 hours last night on what felt like the most comfy mattress I have slept on in a very long time.

I write this whilst looking out of my tent at a hive of activity with skidoos racing around.

After Scott's expedition reached the South Pole, they faced an arduous 800 mile journey to safety and here I am, having flown back, sitting at base camp with warmth, food and medical assistance. How the World has changed over the past 100 years!

The letters from the 'Scott100 letters' competition were processed, and thanks to everyone who took part.

Tomorrow morning I have a live satellite call on Radio Devon at 06:50 GMT and so my alarm is set for a 03:30 local time start. The radio interview is to be repeated tomorrow on BBC TV Spotlight programme

DAY 23

TUE, 08 JAN 2013, 19:25

After spending the past 14 days skiing, I am now trying my hand at other sports here in Antarctica. Last night I participated in an intense game of French cricket, my performance being hindered by my large snow boots. This afternoon I played a game of football alongside South Africans, Argentinians and Australians, with me flying the flag for England. A warm up to the World Cup of 2014 perhaps?

We also used this day to capture more photos of the expedition team. I was dressed in a penguin costume pulling 3 fully laden sledges and a fourth sledge containing Geoff Somers, one of the most accomplished polar travellers in the World. Wow, this place makes you do the strangest things. It certainly amused the Union Glacier residents.

Up at 3:30am local time this morning to speak to BBC Radio Devon. How surreal that interview was, coming 10,000 miles away from the Earth's southernmost continent.

DAY 24
WED, 09 JAN 2013, 15:55

We are due to fly back to Punta Arenas tomorrow and so this is likely to be our last full day in Antarctica. The intention is to fly out in the early hours to avoid the bad weather that is predicted.

After breakfast today I went for a 6 mile ski out of base camp. Whilst doing this, the aches and pains I had become so familiar with during the trek made their reappearance. Yet this time I knew I could turn back at any point to the Union Glacier canteen for tea and biscuits!

I had another live interview with the BBC this evening. After discussing the trek and the aims of the ISCE, it was a lovely surprise when they brought my sister Georgie onto the line!

Although I am very excited to return to the UK and to be reunited with family and friends, I'm definitely going to miss this place and hope that one day I can return. I've certainly caught the polar bug!